To: Dad. Christmas 1971

Peacemakers

W9-DFK-248

You are one of these

love: Keith

In a Broken World

JOHN A. LAPP

EDITOR

HERALD PRESS
Scottdale, Pennsylvania

Happy are those who work
for peace among men:
God will call them his sons!
Matthew 5:9, TEV

This book has been developed jointly by
the Mennonite Church, Scottdale, Pa.,
and the General Conference Mennonite
Church, Newton, Kansas.

PEACEMAKERS IN A BROKEN WORLD

Copyright © 1969 by Herald Press, Scottdale, Pa. 15683
Standard Book Number: 8361-1607-0
Printed in the United States

Design by Gary Gore

Foreword

A fresh voice on peacemaking coming from one of the so-called peace churches has been long overdue in today's warring world. On many occasions the peace witness of the Mennonite Church has suffered due to personal failures within the brotherhood. However, the objectives have never been lost and we still hear the word of Jesus as He speaks to us, "Blessed are the peacemakers: for they shall be called the children of God." As the disciples of Jesus Christ we want to take seriously the role of being peacemakers in a broken world.

Our belief in serving Christ, in mending that which has been broken, in trying to be ministers of reconciliation within the human family, is deeply rooted in nearly 450 years of witnessing for peace. The founders of the Mennonite Church went everywhere preaching the gospel. This brought much suffering and waves of persecution which cost the lives of hundreds. The forefathers stood before magistrates and law officers and prophetically spoke the Word which on many occasions brought guilt to bear upon men's hearts. They spoke against violence and the use of the sword by the executioner and the military forces. The most prolific writer among the Mennonites of the sixteenth century, Menno Simons, noted that "Christ has not taken His kingdom with the sword, but He entered it with much suffering." He said of the followers of Christ, "Hatred and vengeance they did not know, for they love those who hate them; they do good to those who despitefully use them and pray for those who persecute them. . . . Evil they do not repay with evil, but with good. They do not seek merely their own good, but that which is good for their neighbors both as to body and soul. They feed the hungry, give drink to the thirsty, they entertain the needy, release prisoners, visit the sick, comfort the fainthearted, admonish the erring, are ready after their Master's example to give their lives for their brethren."

Today Mennonites discuss among themselves how they should live and witness in a godless, warring world and how to speak to many Christians who do not adhere in the same way to the first principle of the gospel. Ofttimes the question is raised, What should we say to the government? How should we speak to the men of the state? Having enjoyed the blessings of living under a government that has recognized the Christian conscience in time of war, which has not compelled those who could not conscientiously participate in warfare to join the armed forces, has ofttimes made Mennonites a people who are contented with their prosperity and satisfied with the quiet way of life.

Because of this continued need to develop awareness and conviction a series of "Peacemaker Workshops" were held throughout the United States and Canada in the first quarter of 1968. This was followed by a series of eleven Sunday school lessons on "Peacemakers in a Broken World." Many of the papers presented in this book were first presented in "Peacemaker Workshops" throughout the Mennonite brotherhood, sponsored by the Commission for Christian Education and the Committee on Peace and Social Concerns.

Believing that these papers would be stimulating to other persons besides those who attended and that they should also be privileged to benefit from them, we are hereby submitting them to you in this book, edited by John A. Lapp. They are presented as a symposium and primarily express the views of the respective writers. We pray that God may use the messages contained on these pages to stimulate all men to a vital faith in Jesus Christ as our only Savior and Lord, a life which seeks in every experience to be a peacemaker as the disciple of our Lord and to become an active peacemaker in the broken world in which we find ourselves. With the hope that this may be accomplished, we submit this to the readers.

JOHN E. LAPP, *Chairman*
Committee on Peace and Social Concerns
Mennonite Church

Contents

III. VOICES OF HOPE

I

VOICES OF LOVE

1/ BY PETER J. EDIGER

Amos Visits America

Words of Amos

The words of Amos, who was among the shepherds of Tekoa, which he saw concerning Israel in the days of Uzziah king of Judah and in the days of Jeroboam the son of Joash, king of Israel, two years before the earthquake.—1:1.

And he said: "The Lord roars from Zion, and utters his voice from Jerusalem; the pastures of the shepherds mourn, and the top of Carmel withers."—1:2.

Thus says the Lord: "For three transgressions of Damascus, and for four, I will not revoke the punishment; because they have threshed Gilead. . . .

"So I will send a fire upon the house of Hazael, and it shall devour the strongholds of Ben-hadad. I will break the bar of Damascus, and cut off the inhabitants from the Valley of Aven, and him that holds the scepter from Beth-eden; and the people of Syria shall go into exile to Kir," says the Lord.—1:3-5.

Thus says the Lord: "For three transgressions of Gaza, and for four, I will not revoke the punishment; because they carried into exile a whole people to deliver them up to Edom. So I will send a fire upon the wall of Gaza, and it shall devour her strongholds. I will cut off the inhabitants from Ashdod, . . . I will turn

Amos Visits America

The word of Amos which he saw concerning America in the days of Lyndon Johnson, President of the United States, five years after the assassination of President Kennedy.

And he said: "The Lord roars from the city, and from the market-place he utters his voice; so that the people in the suburbs shudder, and even the countryside trembles."

Thus says the Lord: "For three transgressions of China, and for four, I will not withhold the law of harvest; they shall reap what they have sown, because they crushed many people with ruthlessness and closed themselves off from the rest of the world, and sought to stamp out my name with atheistic indocrination; so I will send more purges upon the land, and bloody struggles between leaders of conflicting ideologies and the people of China shall suffer many things," says the Lord.

Thus says the Lord: "For three transgressions of Russia, and for four, I will not withhold the law of harvest; they shall reap what they have sown, because they carried into Siberian exile many who were helpless, breaking up families and destroying villages and severely limiting free expression of views in conflict with the system; so I will send leanness upon the land and sadness upon the people," says the Lord.

my hand against Ekron; and the remnant of the Philistines shall perish," says the Lord.—1:6-8.

Thus says the Lord: "For three transgressions of Tyre, and for four, I will not revoke the punishment; because they delivered up a whole people to Edom, and did not remember the covenant of brotherhood. So I will send a fire upon the wall of Tyre, and it shall devour her strongholds."—1:9, 10.

Thus says the Lord: "For three transgressions of Edom, and four four, I will not revoke the punishment; because he pursued his brother with the sword, and cast off all pity, and his anger tore perpetually, and he kept his wrath for ever. So I will send a fire upon Teman, and it shall devour the strongholds of Bozrah."—1:11, 12.

Thus says the Lord: "For three transgressions of the Ammonites, and for four, I will not revoke the punishment; because they have ripped up women with child in Gilead, that they might enlarge their border. So I will kindle a fire in the wall of Rabbah, and it shall devour her strongholds, with shouting in the day of battle, with a tempest in the day of the whirlwind; and their king shall go into exile, he and his princes together," says the Lord.—1:13-15.

Thus says the Lord: "For three transgressions of Moab, and for four, I will not revoke the punishment; because he burned to lime the bones of the king of Edom. So I will send a fire upon Moab, and it shall devour the strongholds of Kerioth, and Moab shall die amid uproar, amid shouting and the sound of the trumpet; I will cut off the ruler from its midst, and will slay all its princes with him," says the Lord.—2:1-3.

Thus says the Lord: "For three transgressions of Judah, and for four, I will not revoke the punishment; because they have rejected the law of the Lord, and have not kept his statutes, but

Thus says the Lord: "For three transgressions of France, and for four, I will not withhold the law of harvest; they shall reap what they have sown, because they were slow to give up exploitive colonial policies in relationship to emerging nations seeking to boast of fading glory; therefore I will diminish their influence and thwart their ambitions," says the Lord.

Thus says the Lord: "For three transgressions of Germany, and for four, I will not withhold the law of harvest; they shall reap what they have sown, because they succumbed to strong demonic leadership and failed to protest the inhumanity of baking human flesh in ovens and snuffing out millions of lives in gaseous graves; therefore the land will be divided, with a curtain separating brother from brother and mother from daughter."

Thus says the Lord: "For three transgressions of America, and for four, I will not withhold the law of harvest; they shall reap what they have sown, because they did not rise up in protest when their leaders pursued oppressive politics, because they gave silent approval to the raping plunder of a small people already pregnant with problems, because they closed their eyes to the poverty of the poor and turned aside from seeking justice for their brothers to pursuing selfish gain for themselves, because they glorified violence on the screens and in their books, because they placed more value on their objects and their systems than on their neighbors and brothers, because they pursued personal pleasure above personal integrity and social sensitivity."

Now therefore hear this word which the Lord speaks against you, O America; you who have been blessed of all nations of the earth with productivity and affluence and with many churches and much religious activity: "I am holding you accountable for what you do and for what you fail to do."

"Hear, and testify against the religious establishments," says the Lord. "On the day that I punish America for transgressions their lies have led them astray, after which their fathers walked. So I will send a fire upon Judah, and it shall devour the strongholds of Jerusalem."—2:4, 5.

Thus says the Lord: "For three transgressions of Israel, and for four, I will not revoke the punishment; because they sell the righteous for silver, and the needy for a pair of shoes, they that trample the head of the poor into the dust of the earth, and turn aside the way of the afflicted; a man and his father go in to the same maiden, so that my holy name is profaned; they lay themselves down beside every altar upon garments taken in pledge; and in the house of their God they drink the wine of those who have been fined."—2:6-8.

Hear this word that the Lord has spoken against you, O people of Israel, against the whole family which I brought up out of the land of Egypt: "You only have I known of all the families of the earth; therefore I will punish you for all your iniquities." 3:1, 2.

Hear, and testify against the house of Jacob," says the Lord God, the God of hosts, "that on the day I punish Israel for his transgressions, I will punish the altars of Bethel, and the horns of the altar shall be cut off and fall to the ground."—3:13, 14.

"Hear this word, you cows of Bashan, who are in the mountain of Samaria, who oppress the poor, who crush the needy, who say to their husbands, 'Bring, that we may drink!' The Lord God has sworn by his holiness that, behold, the days are coming upon you, when they shall take you away with hooks, even the last of you with fishhooks. And you shall go out through the breaches, every one straight before her; and you shall be cast forth into Harmon," says the Lord.—4:1-3.

"I gave you cleanness of teeth in all your cities, and lack of bread in all your places, yet you did not return to me," says the

I will surely chasten the structures of Christendom and the beautiful sanctuaries shall fall to the ground and the hollow sounds of · your cathedrals shall be heard no more and your altars shall rot in rain."

And then the popular and patriotic preachers of America sent word to Mr. Hoover, director of FBI, saying, "Amos conspired against America. The land is unable to endure all his words. He is guilty of treason."

And the popular and patriotic preachers said to Amos, "O misguided idealist, go away—flee from us. Go back to the Bible and stay there. Don't meddle in our affairs. Go back to the Bible and be a biblical character about whom we can preach in pompous platitudes. Go back to the Bible and stay there. Don't come again to disturb us in 1968."

And Amos said, "I am not a preacher, nor a preacher's son. I am a common laborer in an assembly plant and the Lord spoke to me on an assembly line: 'Go, prophesy to the American people.' And now hear the word of the Lord: 'Unless you repent, your children and children's children shall find no place to hide from bricks nearby and bombs afar.' "

Hear this, you who trample upon the needy and bring the poor into greater economic captivity. I will not forget any of your deeds. Shall not the land tremble when the accounts are settled?

"Behold, the days are coming," says the Lord, "when I will send a famine on the land, not for thirst or bread, but for hearing of the word of the Lord. In mountainous haystacks of religious words they shall seek in vain for the needle of the word of the Lord."

Hear then the word of the Lord, "I'm sick and tired of many of your sacred rites. I am not pleased by your religious rituals.

Lord. "And I also withheld the rain from you when there were yet three months to the harvest; I would send rain upon one city, and send no rain upon another city; one field would be rained upon, and the field on which it did not rain withered; so two or three cities wandered to one city to drink water, and were not satisfied; yet you did not return to me," says the Lord. "I smote you with blight and mildew; I laid waste your gardens and your vineyards; your fig trees and your olive trees the locust devoured; yet you did not return to me," says the Lord. "I sent among you a pestilence after the manner of Egypt; I slew your young men with the sword; I carried away your horses; and I made the stench of your camp go up into your nostrils; yet you did not return to me," says the Lord. "I overthrew some of you, as when God overthrew Sodom and Gomorrah, and you were as a brand plucked out of the burning; yet you did not return to me, says the Lord. "Therefore thus I will do to you. O Israel; because I will do this to you, prepare to meet your God, O Israel!"—4:6-12.

Seek good, and not evil, that you may live; and so the Lord, the God of hosts, will be with you, as you have said. Hate evil, and love good, and establish justice in the gate; it may be that the Lord, the God of hosts, will be gracious to the remnant of Joseph.—5:14, 15.

Woe to you who desire the day of the Lord! Why would you have the day of the Lord? It is darkness, and not light; as if a man fled from a lion, and a bear met him; or went into the house and leaned with his hand against the wall, and a serpent bit him. Is not the day of the Lord darkness, and not light, and gloom with no brightness in it?—5:18-20.

"I hate, I despise your feasts, and I take no delight in your solemn assemblies. Even though you offer me your burnt offerings and cereal offerings, I will not accept them, and the peace offerings of your fatted beasts I will not look upon. Take away from me the noise of your songs; to the melody of your harps I will

14

Even though you offer me a dollar and your fives, or even your fat checks, I will not accept them as an appeasement for your injustice. I do not receive them as cloak to cover the conscience pricks of your insensitivity to the needs of your brother man. But let me tell you what I am looking for. Turn on the stream of justice and let it roll across the land; open irrigation ditches of righteousness and let refreshing waters flood the parched earth of seven continents; turn from the futile pouring of your manhood and your muscle and your money into the outmoded demonic destruction of warfare and channel the idealism and energy and compassion of your people, young and old, into constructive works of righteousness and mercy."

Woe to you who always want to be comfortable in church services, who want to be secure in your well-walled and carpeted religious systems and rely on National Guards and America's massive military might to protect you and your riches and your comfortable religion."

"Woe to you who lie on fancy beds and couches and eat rich foods from well-stocked markets, who delight yourselves with hi-fi stereo music, whose supply of wine is plentiful, and who wouldn't think of missing an appointment at the beauty parlor, but who are not concerned at the needs around you in the world, who do not see, and seeing not, care not, that your brothers are hungry for jobs and food and full humanity."

"Woe to those who do not speak against billions upon billions of military appropriations and reject with a joke an appropriation of millions to eradicate rats in a city slum; they spend more money in one month blasting fire into Vietnamese jungles than it would cost in a year to exterminate rats from their nation's slums."

"Hear this word, you high society girls, you who live in the country club hills, who oppress the weak and ignore the needy, who salve your conscience with lavish parties, where you say to not listen. But let justice roll down like waters, and righteousness like an ever-flowing stream." 5:21-24.

"Woe to those who are at ease in Zion, and to those who feel secure on the mountain of Samaria, the notable men of the first of the nations, to whom the house of Israel come! 6:1.

"Woe to those who lie upon beds of ivory, and stretch themselves upon their couches, and eat lambs from the flock, and calves from the midst of the stall; who sing idle songs to the sound of the harp, and like David invent for themselves instruments of music; who drink wine in bowls, and anoint themselves with the finest oils, but are not grieved over the ruin of Joseph! Therefore they shall now be the first of those to go into exile, and the revelry of those who stretch themselves shall pass away." 6:4-7.

Then Amaziah the priest of Bethel sent to Jeroboam king of Israel, saying, "Amos has conspired against you in the midst of the house of Israel; the land is not able to bear all his words. For thus Amos has said, 'Jeroboam shall die by the sword, and Israel must go into exile away from his land.'" And Amaziah said to Amos, "O seer, go, flee away to the land of Judah, and eat bread there, and prophesy there; but, never again prophesy at Bethel, for it is the king's sanctuary. . . . Then Amos answered Amaziah, "I am no prophet, nor a prophet's son; but I am a herdsman, and a dresser of sycamore trees, and the Lord took me from following the flock, and the Lord said to me, 'Go, prophesy to my people Israel.' Now therefore hear the word of the Lord. . . . Therefore thus says the Lord: 'Your wife shall be a harlot in the city, and your sons and your daughters shall fall by the sword, and your land shall be parceled out by line; you yourself shall die in an unclean land, and Israel shall surely go into exile away from its land.'"—7:10-17.

Hear this, you who trample upon the needy, and bring the poor of the land to an end, saying, "When will the new moon be your domestics, 'Bring on the drinks!' Hear this, you up and climbing middle-class men, who say, 'If they only had my drive, they could better themselves.' Hear this, you up and climbing men and high society girls, the time will come when all you have accumulated will come to naught and all the subtle, legal ways by which your prosperity came at others' expense will be exposed, and your hands will be empty of all save your guilt."

Thus says the Lord: "I sent messengers, but they would not hear. I spoke and spoke, but they would not listen. I sent marchers who walked and walked and talked and talked, but they paid no heed. Therefore," says the Lord, "fires will break out in their cities, and snipers will snipe from the rooftops, and looters will loot your stores, and fear and confusion will reign in the streets. Because you did not hear the voice of the poor and heeded not the marching feet of the oppressed, because you did not know that I was speaking through their voices and walking in their shoes, because you repented not but hardened your hearts in the days when I spoke; therefore I will come with revolution unless you turn and hear your brother's cry and mine."

Thus says the Lord: "Seek good, and not evil, that you may live. Hate evil, and love good, and establish justice in your courts and in legislature halls and in your churches."

Woe to you who glibly say, "We want God's justice; we want God's truth; we want God's judgment." Why would you desire the judgment of God? It is piercing, not pleasant, as if a man fled from a lion and met a bear, or sought shelter in his house from rain and a tornado struck. Is not the judgment of the Lord harsh, with no partiality?

And with those words Amos was about to leave when a reporter asked him for his final statement.

over, that we may sell grain? And the sabbath, that we may offer wheat for sale, that we may make the ephah small and the shekel great, and deal deceitfully with false balances, that we may buy the poor for silver and the needy for a pair of sandals, and sell the refuse of the wheat?" The Lord has sworn by the pride of Jacob: "Surely I will never forget any of their deeds. Shall not the land tremble on this account, and every one mourn who dwells in it, and all of it rise like the Nile . . . of Egypt?"—8:4-8.

"Behold, the days are coming," says the Lord God, "when I will send a famine on the land; not a famine of bread, nor a thirst for water, but of hearing the words of the Lord. They shall wander from sea to sea, and from north to east; they shall run to and fro, to seek the word of the Lord, but they shall not find it."—8:11, 12.

"Are you not like the Ethiopians to me, O people of Israel?" says the Lord. "Did I not bring up Israel from the land of Egypt, and the Philistines from Caphtor and the Syrians from Kir? Behold, the eyes of the Lord God are upon the sinful kingdom, and I will destroy it from the surface of the ground; except that I will not utterly destroy the house of Jacob," says the Lord.—9:7, 8.

"For lo, I will command, and shake the house of Israel among all the nations as one shakes with a sieve, but no pebble shall fall upon the earth. All the sinners of my people shall die by the sword, who say, 'Evil shall not overtake or meet us.' "—9:9, 10.

"Behold, the days are coming," says the Lord, "when the plowman shall overtake the reaper and the treader of grapes him who sows the seed; the mountains shall drip sweet wine, and all the hills shall flow with it. I will restore the fortunes of my people Israel, and they shall rebuild the ruined cities and inhabit them; they shall plant vineyards and drink their wine, and they shall make gardens and eat their fruit. I will plant them upon their land, and they shall never again be plucked up out of the land which I have given them," says the Lord your God.—9:13-15.

And Amos said, "O people of America, thus says the Lord, 'Are you not like Chinese to me, O Americans, and are not the North Vietnamese and South Vietnamese alike to me? Am I not the God of all men? Does not my judgment and love hover over all? the rich and the poor—the oppressor and the oppressed—the haves and the have nots—is any exempt from my judgment or my grace?'"

"Woe to you who can't imagine that God's judgment might come to America, who support the participation in violent upheavals and warfare far away but to whom it is inconceivable that war should come to your front porch." Thus spoke the prophet Amos in his visit to America.

Therefore thus says the Lord, "When you are ready to hear my word and do it, in that day I will renew the falling cities and raise up the ruins of the world. Behold, the day shall come when productivity shall overtake need, and rehabilitation overtake dilapidation, and cities and nations shall be rebuilt, and men shall live in justice and peace."

Thus says the Lord your God. Amen.

2/ BY HUBERT SCHWARTZENTRUBER

The Brokenness of the City

We have access to a little spot of ground in the country. The children can fish and there is a little house on this property. Alongside the house is a pump. The pump has a handle, spout, cylinder, and a pipe going down into a well-drilled well that has plenty of fresh water. Something happened to the pump, however. The iron rod that goes to the cylinder that raises the bucket rusted through and now you can pump and pump, but no water comes. This is frustrating, especially when one is thirsty. There is the pump, the water, and all, but it is not available to me because the pump is broken. In the same way, the moral fiber of our society is rusted through and "fresh" water is difficult to receive.

We live in a society that is connected to rich resources, that could provide abundant living for all, but a vast majority of people go to the pump. and pump, but nothing ever comes. In the same way, the poverty in our nation becomes more severe and little relief is in sight. The machine replaces people faster than new jobs are created. The cost of living soars, but many people have no more income today than they had ten years ago. Some have less.

There has been a lot of talk and some legislation, but there remains a vast amount of segregation, depression, and hopelessness. In spite of the legislation that we have and the many people of good will, segregation and prejudice are becoming harder to face, and as the wounds become greater, the hurt becomes more severe. How long society can survive under this pressure remains to be seen.

The Ghetto Spirit

We moved to St. Louis ten years ago. I know that we did not have any concept of the hopelessness that the ghettos breed. There are no easy answers, yet we say Christ is the answer. There are no outsiders who are experts who can come in with answers for the problems. I do not discredit all the studies made by the social scientist, but most that I am familiar with fall far short of coming close to the roots of the problem. One can really not find answers until he can feel the tense agony and the groans of misery, and the sighs of depression that the ghetto inflicts upon its victims. The man who lives in a continual depression does not need a federal program where millions of dollars are spent to discover his need, and how his problem can be solved. And just before he arrives at a solution the money runs out and the poor man is in a worse dilemma than he was before. Now he is also angry at the man who got the money that was intended for him. He again is left with no assurance that his situation will ever become any better.

I traveled through Fulton, Missouri, recently. It was there that Winston Churchill phrased the famous term "Iron Curtain." I am sure that Churchill sensed the devastation that any artificial wall that divides people can bring. But long before World War II days, another kind of curtain had already fallen. This curtain was made from a fabric of fear, suspicion, and misinformation. Into it was woven hate, prejudice, greed, and selfishness. It was erected by many people. The church shared in the task. Men greedy for gain helped. The banker and the groceryman helped. Big industry also supplied some material. Little ordinary people helped to gather together a lot of the materials to make the curtain. Everybody had a part. The curtain fell while the church was sleeping. But then why should she not sleep? She has loudly proclaimed that there is no relationship with man's physical needs and the gospel. But now in the lateness of the hour, we are ready to admit that we were wrong and that all of man's concerns are spiritual concerns and the business of the church is to be servant to all. But it is very late. Perhaps too late.

When the monstrous curtain fell to divide people and fence them in, prisons such as history has never known before were developed. Some of the great religious awakenings of history occurred when God's people became interested in finding ways of bringing hope to a segment of society suffering from oppression. Today the literal flames of hell are seen burning in our poverty-stricken areas. The gnashing of teeth is not an unfamiliar sound, and the voices crying for a cup of cold water can be heard almost everywhere.

In the Ghetto

Recently a man told me that his son was threatened with a knife and gun by a group of boys playing basketball on the cement slab behind the church. His son ran home to get the butcher knife to fight it out. And his intentions were for real. This man's son is no different from any average boy. He has abilities to do well in school and with a little coaching can readily learn new skills. We say how awful that he would run home and get the knife. But let us not be too critical of his decision to get a knife, until we can feel and learn some of the facts.

For all of his fifteen years he wore clothing that the white woman, whom his mother worked for, gave to them. For five days a week his mother needs to get up at 5:00 a.m., and get her nine children ready for school and then ride the bus for an hour and a half to the country to wash clothes, clean windows, scrub floors, and wash dirty dishes, and then return late at night having made barely $1.00 per hour that day. Many families with ten children have less than $3,000 income per year.

The father too has his problems. He wants, like nothing else in the world, to be the breadwinner and the provider of his household. He has worked hard all day sweeping cigarette butts at Union Station and sweeping floors in the tavern to make a few pennies. When he was growing up there were no other jobs. His white brother with the same education and no more skills got the better jobs. After both parents work hard and still see no relief in sight they finally give up trying. He stomps out of the house and goes to the tavern; she lives with the hungry children, shoeless and friendless. He finds no one who understands him. He is told to pull himself up by his bootstraps, but there aren't any bootstraps left on his boots.

He pays exorbitant interest on money he needs to borrow. The house he rents is higher priced than his white brother's but in much poorer condition. It is bad before he gets it and he is then blamed for letting it go down. If you don't believe in a hell, let me take you to some hovels where human souls are literally rotting away.

One lady told me once in a church membership class: "My income does not keep our children fed and clothed, and so I supplement my income by selling my body to men." What mother can stand the sight of her children hungry to the point of starvation? Who commits the greater sin, the woman who sells her body or the society that forces her to do it? Before we become judgmental, let us understand the facts. It is imperative we stop trying to treat cancer with aspirins.

The fifteen-year-old boy with the butcher knife has other problems too. He and forty-eight other children share the same classroom. He uses books that are no longer good enough to use in the suburban schools. The teacher could really not teach forty-eight children; so all she can do is baby-sit till the bell rings and then send the children home. Finally he graduates from school and goes on to high school. He can barely compete with fifth graders. Soon he decides school is not for him.

The Sources of Bitterness

There are a number of reasons why he decides to drop out. He is tired of eating the warmed over french fries that are left over from the schools in the plush community. He has never been treated like a man and so why should he now all of a sudden act like one? He knows that jobs aren't available for him. If he wants to do anything, it will likely be to serve as a porter like his father, sweeping the white man's cigarette butts at Union Station. Finally he decides that he may as well quit. After all, life will never have anything for him. His parents were starved out in the South. The machine could pick cotton faster than they could and so the machine had more value than they had. His father never had a chance. His father before him had no more of a chance, and his father before him was being beaten with horse whips and sold on the auction block like a hog. And his parents before him were captured like wild turkeys and stacked three deep in slave boats and floated across the ocean like pine logs and sold for a price to "Christians." Their wives and sweethearts were torn asunder. Children were torn from their mothers' breasts. Some became only breeding stock. Some became victims of lustful owners.

I know a lady who is over 100 years old now. She is a friend of some members of our congregation. I talked to her one day and she started to tell me some things about life on the plantation. Her father was a slave. She told me one thing that she will always remember about her father: even in his later years, after a hard day's work, he would come into the house, sit at the kitchen table, and put his head in his hands and cry. In his sobs he would say, "They sold my mother; they sold my mother."

Wounds of this dimension do not heal easily. And it takes more than one generation. Today, the fifteen-year-old boy with the butcher knife is still suffering from this wound, and never let yourself believe that it isn't so.

He starts hanging around on the street with the other boys who have come to the same conclusion sooner than he did. They are introduced to marihuana. A white peddler gave them some to try and then gets them hooked. They soon need to steal to get money to buy the drug. Soon he has a prison record and no job is available anymore. He sees the error of his way, but where can he go for help? When he goes for a job, he is told that the position has just been filled. He walks down the street and sees a white boy go in and then the job is available again. Finally he gives up, never to try again.

On television he sees the black boys get murdered in Vietnam. Why try to protect a country that in his mind is only fit for burning? A few black power advocates incite him to riot, and loot, and burn. Why should he not do it? This is the first time that he could prove that he is a man. After all, he has nothing to lose. He has suffered so long now it is his turn to retaliate.

He has so often heard the landlord promise to make repairs without any intentions of doing so. He sees the bill collector take the last dollar out of the house to pay for a product that some greedy salesman sold them on time payments. He remembers when the church retreated to the greener pastures where the offering would be larger on a Sunday morning. He knows full well that the dim lights on the streets are also a symbol of the dim attitudes and little concerns that are shared with him. He has so often heard the politician make promises but never seen him make any of them good. He has seen the welfare agencies despise him. He has seen policemen shoot and kill his buddy while he sits handcuffed in the back seat of a police car. He knows what it is like to be chased out of "good" neighborhoods. He knows what it means to be robbed of all his dignity. He knows what it is like to be last in everything.

All of us were tense last summer when the Rap Browns and the Stokely Carmichaels were burning up cities. Many people, however, are putting the blame on the wrong people. Stokely Carmichael, H. Rap Brown, or anyone else cannot start a riot and burn a city without the fermenting tensions of years and years. It is not the black power people that are burning our cities. It is the power of the white noose that has been around the neck of the ghetto for so long a period of time squeezing the very breath out of the people. It is the time of harvest for the injustices that have been heaped upon a segment of society for so long a time.

The Ghetto Disorder

The term "ghetto" was used to define the Jewish quarter in sixteenth-century Venice. America has used the term for the areas that are restricted to people for a certain skin color, and limited their freedom of choice. The characteristics of the ghetto are over-

25

crowding, deteriorated housing, high infant mortality, crime, and disease. This breeds hostility, despair, apathy, self-depreciation, and grandiose behavior.

Yet among the conglomeration and upheaval and disorder there is an order all of its own. There is a language that is commonly understood. There is a certain way of doing things. One must filter out some things he hears and interpret them in his own way.

The ghettos perpetuate themselves through their increasing ugliness, deterioration, and isolation which strengthen the Negro's sense of worthlessness and impotence. Although the white affluent community is blind to what goes on in the ghetto, the ghetto dweller is not blind to what goes on in the white community. By means of television he knows what is going on in the white community which only adds to the hurt.

While many find positive ways to get out of their depression by fighting all odds, getting an education, a job, and a satisfying homelife, usually the positive attitudes are formed because of the interest of a teacher, pastor, community worker, or some other friend who encourages and walks with them during the struggling years.

But many more become overt delinquents or self-conscious rebels seeking a solution in defiant, aggressive, and finally self-destroying behavior. He argues that he cannot hope to win meaningful self-esteem through the avenues ordinarily available to most people. The social and political power is not responsive to his need.

Community action is becoming alive in the ghetto, suggesting that there is still a reservoir of energy ready to be stirred. Effective protest cannot arise out of total stagnation, though protest and demonstrations run the risk of becoming only a safety valve without transforming society. When no heed is given to the protests to the point where society is changed, then the depression becomes sealed in bomb shells that will later erupt violently.

There are many indications to believe that violence of the past was a picnic compared to what may yet take place. No one is poor because he is white, but many are poor because they are black.

Hard core slums are the result of continued deterioration. People with jobs and skills move out. These are replaced by new migrants who have no jobs, are not eligible for public assistance, live with relatives until they qualify for aid. They are trapped by a history of degradation and impact of automation, unavailability of low and middle income housing, and color discrimination. This forces people to a level of existence that is not human.

There is no place in the world where it hurts more to be poor than in the ghettos of our American cities. The man in the ghetto is tortured like a hungry dog that is chained, and outside of the reach of his chain is meat that would satisfy his hunger but there is no hope of ever getting it. So he starves to death while he looks at the very thing that would keep him alive. This is what our society is doing to the captives in the prisons of the ghetto.

The problems continue to mount. Each year America has 2.7 million more people. This means each year we have one new city the size of the metropolitan area of St. Louis. Between 1940 and 1967, 4,000,000 Negroes moved from the rural south to the northern and western cities. America annually spends $75 billion for defense but allots only $7 billion for welfare. We spent $17.4 billion on tobacco and liquor, but $1.6 billion on the war on poverty. We spent $3.2 billion on cosmetics and toiletries but only $400 million to train unemployed adults.

The chances are one to six that the 200 millionth person born in America was black. The odds are even that he will live part of his childhood in a broken home; three chances out of five that he will live on public welfare; two chances out of five that he will drop out of school.

In our St. Louis ghetto 15 percent of employable males are unemployed, 50 percent of out-of-school teenagers are unemployed, 7 percent of those with jobs do not work full time, 20 percent of those working full time earned less than $60 per week, 40 percent of the families earn less than $3,000 per year, when the present cost of maintaining a modest standard of living for a family of four is $7,000 per year. Over 70 percent of families in ghetto fall into the below-the-necessary minimum for decent standard of living. Can we now understand the results: poor housing, inadequate diet, poor medical care, few books or magazines, and the despair?

The Church's Response

In light of the threat of much more violence and bloodshed and the backlash of corrupt political systems and machines, what does the church have to say?

Perhaps we are now on the threshold of another great religious awakening, when God will walk through the ghettos and all segments of broken society, in His church, and shed new light on the dark streets and glass-strewn alleys.

Jesus said, "The Spirit of the Lord is upon me, because he hath anointed me to preach the gospel to the poor; he hath sent me to heal the brokenhearted, to preach deliverance to the captives, and recovering of sight to the blind, to set at liberty them that are bruised, to preach the acceptable year of the Lord" (Luke 4:18, 19).

If we, His body on earth, are here to carry out His ministry, then this very ministry is ours too. What is the gospel, the good news that we preach? If we lead a person to a knowledge of Christ as Savior and then send him with a hungry stomach and diseased body because of lack of proper medical care; or send him back to a house that is falling down, where the children eat plaster and die from lead poisoning, and stairways are crumbling and every room a fire trap; and say God bless you, we have missed the meaning of the gospel. What good news is there when I can't get a job and my children get second-rate education and everybody uses me as a stepping-stone for their own advancement?

We must make an attempt to relieve these conditions with a Christian compassion for all those in distress. I get letters in the mail encouraging me to relax from this kind of "social gospel" type of ministry. Nothing is more important to me than a relationship with God that frees man from sin and guilt and establishes a relationship that has deeper meaning than any ties on earth. Yet the ministry to a man's physical needs comes in the same

28

package. It is not preaching first and then serving the material needs, nor is it serving the material needs and then preaching. What we do, we do out of a motivation of love and obedience to Jesus Christ.

There are many needs to which the church must address itself if we are going to even save ourselves. We must give attention to the plight of humanity in the urban ghettos. The isolated rural poor need a spokesman. The man that has lost hope in society and sees no way out. The man that sees the church in the same light as all other power structures where it has become a clique all eating at the same trough and getting fatter. The man that because of all this has also lost faith in God.

I conclude by affirming that the gospel is good news which frees a man to be a person as God intended him to be. Jesus Christ is the answer, but when I affirm this, I must be willing to place myself in a position where He can use me to be the answer. This can happen only when I am in constant relationship with God that the Holy Spirit can work through my life.

This can happen only when I am close enough to the stress of human suffering that at a moment's notice God can say to me: "Come, bear the cross with your brother here." Or are we so far away that God can never reach us?

3/ BY C. NORMAN KRAUS

Christian Perspectives on Nationalism, Racism, and Poverty in American Life

To give a detailed analysis of the problem mentioned in the title is not my intention. Mine is the far less pretentious task of sharing some reflective observations on the nature, causes, and possible solutions of these problems. My hope is that these cursory comments and the interpretation suggested will invite further inquiry.

Nationalism Defined

That nationalism should be listed as a problem at all will surprise some readers. Patriotism, appreciation for, and loyalty to one's nation are certainly praiseworthy. National association and political organization provide a means of identity and a sense of belonging for citizens. National commonality provides a basis for cooperative economic and political action. National loyalty provides motivation for effort and sacrifice, in behalf of the larger social group. Obviously these things are good.

The national state is a body of people associated together within a given territory, bound together by cultural, ethnic, and historical similarities, and joined together in a political and military alliance and organization. The nation is a larger and in many respects more impersonal social unit than the family or clan, but it has much the same dynamic or power over the individual. It has a collective ego, and unfortunately it displays many of the selfish and unworthy aspects of the individual ego.

To put it another way, the individual often identifies himself

30

with the collective ego, and in the name of patriotism justifies selfish and discriminatory action. The "me first" instinct is blown up and justified in terms of the national group interest. And in this same spirit the interests of the nation are viewed as separate from and in competition with other nations.

Characteristics of Self-Centered Nationalism

This kind of self-centered nationalism is called chauvinism. When this kind of group selfishness puts national interests ahead of the needs and aspirations of other weaker nations and insists on its own rights and privileges even to the disadvantage of such nations, then it has become a problem. Christians cannot justify selfishness, either on an individual or national level.

Our problem is to identify such selfish nationalism and disassociate ourselves from it. Thus it becomes necessary to recognize some of the common traits which characterize illegitimate nationalism.

First and most characteristic is an excessive appeal to patriotism and the ideals of the nation. Chauvinistic appeals often advocate and play upon national pride. They make liberal use of patriotic slogans such as "freedom" or "the right to private property." They advocate aggressive self-defense, and are generally pro-militaristic.

But usually one will find in such appeals a hidden if not apparent self-contradiction. In the name of freedom these appeals are quick to undercut the freedom of others. In the name of "rights" they are callous to the rights of others. And in order to establish their own position they are quick to accuse those who differ with them on social or political issues of disloyalty to the nation. The catchall epithets for their opponents are "liberal," and even more common "communist."

A second characteristic of much illegitimate nationalism is its appeal to the "old-fashioned religion." It comes in the guise of "God and country" and often presents itself as a movement "back to the Bible." It labels its ethic Christian morality and deplores the growth of crime in the streets and the breakdown of the family.

For example, Howard Kershner who publishes a paper called *Christian Economics* wrote in a recent issue: "I am sure we all want to maintain the basic spiritual and economic principles laid down by our founding fathers. . . . To preserve our freedom, our free government and to pass them on to our children, we defend the Constitution, the Bill of Rights, and our religious heritage." The Ku Klux Klan has for its theme song, "The Old Rugged Cross." Many other illustrations could be listed.

This is not to slur the Bible or Christian morality, but to point out that nationalists frequently use religious slogans and techniques as emotional weapons to coerce their listeners into agreement with their political and economic views. They misuse the Bible for selfish, nationalistic ends. They imply that if one disagrees with them in their social and political philosophy he is against the Bible.

A third characteristic of overzealous nationalists is their great oversimplification of the international situation. They tend to divide the world into two camps—the "free world" and the "communist world." They tend to see all international political issues as black and white, and identify the opponent with evil and the devil. From this perspective such nationalism is almost always against the United Nations and against any foreign aid. "Why," they ask rhetorically, "should our nation continue to help nations that are lazy and unappreciative? Why should we help our enemies?"

Oversimplification leads to the constant use of stereotypes, epithets, and simplistic definitions. All shades and types of political liberals are simply identified as communists. All Negro leaders are classified as violent black power advocates. As one who represents this position puts it, "Martin Luther King, Rap Brown, Stokely Carmichael, and the communists are all in the same boat so far as I am concerned. I don't think there is any difference between them." All conscientious objectors are peaceniks, yellow bellies, draft card burners, and unpatriotic. Conversely such simplistic thinking generally leads to the unqualified identification of the right with "our side." Our side is white, right, and free. The enemy is black, or at least colored, sinister, and enslaved.

Finally, chauvinistic thinking appeals to the idea that might makes right. This appeal rests on the assumptions that America is strong because it is right, and thus it has the responsibility to use its might to enforce its righteousness on the rest of the world. It advocates a strong military arsenal and increased police strength in order to deal with the revolutions and riots which inflict our world today. Accordingly, the whole solution to race riots is more police, armored tanks, guns, and tear gas. The solution to Vietnam is nuclear weapons and hundreds of thousands more troops.

I have attempted to give several objectional characteristics of extreme nationalism without giving many illustrations of it. Analysis of publications like the *Dan Smoot Report*, "Manion Forum" (radio program), *Liberty Lobby, American Opinion, Christian Economics*, and *The Christian Beacon*, as well as syndicated columns by men like David Lawrence, Ralph de Toledano, and Holmes Alexander will provide further examples.

Christians put Christ ahead of the nation. They see all men as God's creatures and men for whom Christ died. Their compassion and goodwill involve no national boundaries. They refuse to draw lines on the basis of color, nation, and race where men are in need. They never subscribe to the theory that might makes right, but view their own nation as well as others in the light of God's law and His judgment. While Christians do not expect political organizations to bring in the kingdom of God, it would seem consistent to welcome, encourage, and cooperate with all organizations which genuinely work for world betterment and world peace.

Racism--Continues in the United States

Racism continues to be a problem in the United States. In the last five years the situation in the struggle for civil rights has changed significantly, but white racism as so eloquently pointed out in the *Report of the National Advisory Commission on Civil Disorders*, remains the core of the problem. Racism sounds like such an ugly word that no one wants to admit to himself that he is a racist. But a racist is not necessarily a mean, vile person who wishes others dead or deported. Of course, there are that kind of racists, but they are relatively few. By far the largest group of racists are upstanding patriotic people who are good neighbors and kindhearted parents.

Essentially a racist is one who believes that there are some inherent differences between the different human racial stocks which make some groups better than others. There is still the widespread opinion abroad in America that some races are more intelligent, more morally sensitive, more energetic and self-reliant than others.

But there are degrees of racism. There are some who might hesitate to say that whites are inherently superior to Negroes or Mongolians; however, they would hold that the so-called racial differences between human beings are significant enough that society should recognize them and be organized accordingly. Racists in this second category still hold to the old "separate but equal" doctrine.

It is people holding to these notions who continue to drag their feet and make excuses. They do not favor integrated housing. They are fearful about black and white children going to school together. They want Negroes to have better chances and a higher standard of living, but they want them to stay with their "own people" and not threaten the security of the white community. These are the people which the President's Riot Commission Report names as the "core of the problem," and unfortunately they still control the pulpits and church boards in many of the churches in America.

It is absolutely imperative that the church affirm in clear and certain terms the biblical teaching that the human race is one race, not three races. It is even more imperative that the church begin to live up to its creed. It has been fourteen years since the Supreme Court handed down its decision about school desegregation, but still there has been no determined outcry from the churches demanding that the discrimination and injustice of the past be corrected. Indeed, the white churches as a whole have not given moral leadership in any area of the struggle to end discrimination. Even today it remains true as Walter Reuther said over a decade ago that eleven o'clock Sunday morning is the most segregated hour of the week.

34

The change in the civil rights movement from 1963 to 1968 can be described as a shift in emphasis from integration to black power. This is not a total change, but there are significant differences and they call for a reevaluation of the white Christian's role in the struggle of a just social order. Black power is viewed by many in the white community as simply black violence, and to be sure there is a violent fringe in the black community. But we should keep in mind that there is and has been for years a violent fringe in the white community. Further, all the evidence suggests that the large majority of the Negro community is against violence. The many notable and successful attempts of Negro youth as well as the adult leaders to "cool it" during the explosive week following Martin Luther King's assassination are good evidence of this.

Just now it is crucial that responsible people in both the white and black communities should work for understanding and continuing cooperations.

Black Power Goals

In order to properly assess the changed situation we need to understand what black power means. The advocates of black power have three basic goals.

First, black power seeks to give the black citizens of America a satisfying self-identity. They are trying to reverse a longtime feeling of inferiority and depreciation of blackness in the Negro community. One has only to look at old issues of a magazine like *Ebony* to see that it was the light-colored Negro who was idealized. The black community had absorbed the white community's prejudices. It had accepted the white man's view of itself as second-class. Black power says this must be changed. The black man must respect his blackness. He must know and appreciate his own history and culture. He must stop being a "nobody" and assert himself as "somebody."

Second, the advocates of black power are attempting to give the black community a new sense of cohesion as a community. Negro society is torn apart by the same economic and social stratification which exists in the white community. In addition there are the added strains caused by middle- and upper-class Negroes attempting to gain status with the white majority. Whites usually have assumed that Negroes are a close-knit group. But this is not true. In the early days of the civil rights movement the divisiveness in the Negro community was a major problem. Negro groups farther up the social and economic ladder were threatened by the demonstrations as much as were the whites. Black power is working to weld the black citizens into a self-conscious cooperative group which can and will stand together in the fight for justice.

Finally, black power aims to develop both a political and economic power bloc. In order to be able to bargain with the white power structures—industry, business, and government—such a power bloc is believed essential. Some examples of this kind of power will help us to understand their work.

In the Negro ghetto grocery chain stores sell inferior goods at higher prices than whites have to pay. Leftover vegetables gathered from stores in predominantly white neighborhoods are taken to the ghetto for sale. Poor people trapped in these ghettos must pay higher prices for inferior goods. Without cooperative, coordinated effort this kind of inequity cannot be stopped. Black power advocates intend to stop it.

In far too many of our American cities, governments have failed to make any concentrated effort at bettering the conditions in the Negro ghetto. Indeed, in far too many cases conditions are worse today than they were ten years ago in spite of all the civil rights movement has tried to do. Promises have been made and broken many times over the years. White landowners charge high rents and refuse to repair dilapidated buildings. Public services such as garbage collection and street sweeping are inadequate. Until Negro citizens work together as a political group these conditions are not remedied. Black power advocates intend to see them remedied.

Black power can be both good and bad. If it gives the Negro a new sense of self-respect and dignity as a human being, it will be very good. And it will make possible a new day in race relations. If, on the other hand, it creates a new kind of racism in reverse and polarizes the white and Negro communities, it can only do great harm.

The road ahead will inevitably be very difficult. As the black minority struggles for a new self-understanding and a new role in American society, it is likely to seem alternatively aggressive in its demands for more and unwilling to accept what is offered in good faith. It is most likely to demand a greater degree of integration into American society while at the same time showing increased signs of black separatism. Great patience will be needed on both sides before the wounds of the past have healed.

The Church and Poverty

The problems of poverty and race are closely related and intertwined. The Negro minority in America constitutes one of the largest poverty blocs. The percentage of unemployment among the Negroes is regularly at least twice that of the white community. Discrimination in employment keeps blacks at lower paying jobs and pays them less for doing the same kind of work done by their white colleagues. But there are many other poor in America, and the gap between the rich and the poor has been widening despite the fact that our overall living standard and take-home pay has risen.

Our task is not to discuss the problem of poverty per se but rather to see how churches have traditionally viewed the problem of poverty and suggest some reasons why it is necessary to change our attitudes. Indeed, we need a change of viewpoint in order to even tackle the contemporary problem of poverty.

Almost any good church member can quote the words of Jesus, "The poor you have always with you." It is quite commonly assumed by the religious communities of America that poverty like wars will be a part of the human predicament until the end of the age. Many hardworking church members feel little if any responsibility to work at the poverty problem beyond the occasional giving of alms or sharing with the neighboring family hit by calamity.

Traditionally evangelical Christianity in America has viewed poverty as a problem not of society but of the individual. Further, with the exception of those unable to work, poverty like drunkenness has been considered a blameworthy condition in which to be found. It was generally assumed that the poor were either lazy, shiftless, poor managers, or spendthrifts, and a second Bible verse almost universally known was, "If a man will not work, neither shall he eat."

The church promoted an ethic of work and thrift; and it subscribed to the theory that the cure for poverty is good hard work. Dwight L. Moody, the great evangelist, once said that any man could get ahead in life if he would just work with greater diligence. He thought that ever more diligent work was the solution to low wages. Surely the employer would reward hard work. The burden of proof was on the laborer. Henry Ward Beecher, the great public orator and a social liberal of the late nineteenth century, also assumed that the burden of proof lay on the worker. If he could make only a dollar a day, Beecher said, then he should live within his means. He once said that a dollar a day should be sufficient to keep a family of six. It would, he said, buy bread and water was free. And he added, "A man that cannot live on bread and water is not fit to live."

For those whom we might call the innocent poor the church prescribed charity. for the rest it prescribed salvation and moral reform. Assuming that poverty was caused by moral weakness, the church with the exception of those who preached the "social gospel" asserted that if it could persuade a man to accept Jesus, that would take care of his problem.

Today it is much more evident to us that poverty is a social problem. It is caused by convulsions in the social and economic life of the nation and not merely by individual lack of initiative and enterprise. The coincidence of the technical revolution, the racial revolution, and the population explosion have put many who would like to work out of a job. Automation and other advanced technical developments have threatened the jobs of thousands. Labor unions have worked hard to protect the jobs of men being replaced by new machines. Some of their solutions like featherbedding on the railroads seem artificial and are probably unsatisfactory for the long run, but they do point to one aspect of the poverty problem. In Calcutta, India, where the population explosion heightens the unemployment problem still further, the emerging labor unions were advocating "Ban automation." In Chicago, where racial discrimination greatly increases the problem, hundreds of Negroes in a demonstration were chanting alternately "We want work" and "We want food."

Varied Causes of Poverty

The poor in the United States have been classified according to the various causes of poverty. A brief look at some of these classifications will help us to see the many dimensions of the contemporary problem. There are, first of all, the "case poor." These are the physically and mentally disabled, and they are relatively few in number. Public charity and specialized work and rehabilitation programs will continue to be necessary for them.

Then there are what John Kenneth Galbraith has called the "insular poor." These are the people who are trapped in the "islands of poverty" like the Allegheny Mountains where once flourishing coal mines have been closed for years.

Third, there are the racial and ethnic poor. These people are caught for reasons beyond their control in a situation where work is at least sporadic and wages are low. Illustrative of this group are the hundreds of Negro men who daily gather on Pettigrew Street in Durham, North Carolina, and wait for someone who needs unskilled labor to hire them for the day. Often large numbers of men stand idle waiting all day and come back the next morning hoping for better things another day. Most large southern cities have their "Pettigrew Streets."

Fourth, there are the displaced poor such as the farm laborers of the South who have been displaced by machine in the first instance and then geographically displaced in the large cities of the nation where they have moved to find work and a new life. They are in more ways than one "displaced persons"—uprooted and lost in a society which has no work for them.

Then there are the migrant poor who follow the harvest from place to place working for minimal wages and too often exploited by their employers. There are an increasing number of what we might call "middle aged" poor. These are people who have worked for the first half of their wage-earning lives in a factory only to be laid off because of a shutdown. These people in the 40-to-65-year-old bracket find it very difficult to relocate and sometimes go for years without finding steady work.

Lastly, I will mention the so-called "hard core unemployed." These people introduce us to another aspect of the poverty problem. They are the products of long-standing unemployment; for example, families which have been on relief for many years, men and women who have grown up in the slums and ghettos where they have been victims of cultural poverty, unstable homes, and long-standing discrimination and despair. Caught in a vicious circle they have become psychologically unable to hold a steady job. They lack the motivation and discipline to work.

There are, of course, other causes, and many of the causes which we have mentioned overlap to produce even more complex circumstances. But enough has been said to show that poverty is a social problem with psychological and cultural aspects as well as economic factors. This means that the remedy for poverty will have to include far more than sporadic gifts of charity, relief programs, or even government unemployment insurance programs. Christians who care and would serve "in the name of Christ" must consider seriously whether the command to "do good unto all men" does not require them to move beyond the conventional relief measures to work at the causes of poverty.

Toward Some Solutions

But what can we do? To begin with there are no solutions without far more effort and sacrifice than affluent Americans have been willing to make up to this time. Paul A. Miller, former president of the University of West Virginia and more recently a staff member of the Department of Health, Education, and Welfare, said in a speech at Goshen College that the hard fact up to now is that we have not been willing to forego the extra television set, the second car, or an extension to the house, in order to make it possible to balance the economic scales of justice.

Individuals can prepare themselves in social work and in specialized areas of education which will qualify them to work at the problems of the poor.

Enterprising businessmen and industrialists can help by locating new industry in depressed areas. Certainly the Christian businessman will not make large profits if his first concern is where he can be of genuine service to others in need. Although it should be so obvious as not to need mention, Christian employers should pay fair wages rather than the minimum in the area. Especially should employers be sensitive to the needs of the disadvantaged such as migrants. To take advantage of "cheap labor" in order to make greater profits is a denial of Christian love. In addition all of us work for fair employment practices and an end to discriminatory hiring in our communities.

Having said this, however, we must recognize that a problem of this proportion cannot be solved without creative government action. Industry and big business by themselves cannot or at least have not to date done much to remedy the situation. Unfortunately it has not been in the nature of a capitalistic system to voluntarily work out solutions to the kinds of problems we have just reviewed. In fact, historically it has been necessary for government to legislate minimum wages, fair employment practices, unemployment compensation, and the like. And by and large it has been under the pressure of the organized labor movements that business and industry have come to accept social responsibility.

To correct the contemporary injustice will take the kind of concerted, coordinated effort and the large amounts of money which only the government can supply through taxation. The problem is much larger than church and private organizations can handle. This does not mean that government alone can do it; rather, there must be a coordinated effort among government, industry, and the churches. The government itself realizes this. The federal government has specifically appealed to industry to take a more aggressive role in the solution of our contemporary problems, and in several areas there has been a significant response on the part of industry. When the Office of Economic Opportunity and the VISTA programs were first opened in the federal government's "war on poverty," the government openly welcomed the churches' cooperation and willingly supplied funds without inhibitive controls for religious groups who were willing to help.

If what I have said about the need for government action is correct, then it follows that we should be ready to cooperate in every way possible with our government. We should support legislation in this field. We should be willing to pay the taxes necessary to fund programs that are needed. And we might well be ready to work at the grass roots in government-related programs. Indeed, the success of such programs at the grass roots is directly dependent upon the integrity and competence of the persons who are actually involved doing the work.

Let us willingly lay aside our old biases and old inadequate solutions to new and gigantic problems, and by the grace and spirit of our Lord give ourselves with renewed vigor to the service of our fellowmen and witness to our Lord Jesus Christ.

4/ BY R. HERBERT MINNICH

Hunger, Revolution, and the Church

Hunger and revolution? Both are present in many parts of our world and both will increase during the next decade. The role of the church is currently ambiguous in relation to both hunger and revolution. Encouraging changes, however, are taking place among both Roman Catholics and Protestants which indicate that Christian concern is growing about meeting the needs of hungry men and women who have suffered economic, social, political, and spiritual injustices for generations.

The three major world areas which may be generally described as "underdeveloped" are Asia, Africa, and Latin America. In 1963 a study of dietary deficiencies throughout the world indicated that the proportion of the population living in countries with average caloric intakes below the FAO (Food and Agricultural Organization of the United Nations) recommended minimum level of 2,550 was 92 percent for Asia, 38 percent for Africa, and 29 percent for Latin America.

Hunger in Latin America

To say that about 30 percent of the people in Latin America have deficient diets is to average out widely differing situations. In terms of entire countries, recent data indicate that Peru and Colombia have a daily per capita calorie level similar to China (2,177) and those of Ecuador (1,916) and Bolivia (1,814) are lower than that of India (2,029)! In these countries hunger is the daily experience of the great majority of the population. Hardworking

43

Indian porters chew coca leaves to deaden hunger pains, a habit shared by a large proportion of the Andean Indian population.

During the 1960's the picture has definitely darkened. Since 1961 the FAO has reported a steady decline in per capita food production. Due to continued population growth, this lack of increase in agricultural production means a net loss in per capita food production. Inasmuch as hunger was a problem in 1950 in much of Latin America, "diet-deficit" regions are now more seriously deficient than eighteen years ago. Of course, some areas have seen an improvement in food resources, which means that the more backward regions and nations have suffered a larger net decline in per capita food production than the generalized statistics indicate. In Brazil the 1966 production of rice dropped 35 percent, potatoes 36 percent, and beans 34 percent, from the 1965 levels.

Sociocultural Factors Affecting Hunger

One explanation of this abnormal situation relates to the *system of farming*. Throughout Latin America one can see peasants tilling the soil with tools similar to those used in Egypt in the days of Moses. Man is still used as a beast of burden, and millions of peasants continue to use the hoe and machete as their principal tools. From Mexico to southern South America one may find large areas where primitive "fire agriculture" is still practiced. A tract of timber is felled, the dried trees and underbrush are burned, and then beans, rice, manioc, and corn are planted among the charred stumps. A fantastic amount of effort is required to prepare a small clearing whose fertility is lost in two or three years, and the destructive process is then repeated.

During the latter part of the dry season I have flown for hundreds of miles in central Brazil through a haze of smoke in which one rarely could see either sky or soil from an altitude of 1,000 feet. The sun remained a red ball throughout the day. This "slash and burn" system of agriculture holds large areas in a bondage of hunger and perpetual poverty. Such a system of farming is characterized by a lack of knowledge and techniques to achieve the levels of food production needed to eradicate hunger.

The *large-estate system*, or plantation pattern, is a second sociocultural factor affecting the hunger problem in Latin America. Wherever the plantation has flourished in the New World, we find the type of social system which encourages the development of a small, elite owner class and a large, low-prestige laborer class. The large-estate system continues to rely upon "cheap labor," and the resultant hunger and poverty is easily documented in the United States as well as in much of Latin America. Hunger and malnutrition in the Mississippi Delta country, for example, is well known. Children still die or are permanently injured by a lack of food, a paucity of proteins, vitamins, and minerals.

Workers on the plantations frequently are forced to buy from the company store, and in parts of Brazil the author has been told that small vegetable gardens are forbidden, or must be planted on infertile ground. The reason given is that good land must not be taken out of cash-crop production! Thus the domination of the workers by the owners and their supervisors contributes to the problem of hunger, and of an adequate, balanced diet in such large-estate regions. On the traditional large estate, prestige has been associated with the amount of land owned, rather than the level of production achieved.

A third sociocultural factor related to the problem of hunger in Latin America is the large *migration of rural people to the cities.* This "rural-urban exodus" is taking hundreds of thousands of persons into urban environments where they lack marketable skills. In addition, the migration causes a loss of workers on estates which frequently are still dependent upon a large supply of cheap laborers. These "displaced persons" are drawn to the cities by the reports of a better life which they believe they will find there. As a result, burgeoning urban slums encircle the cities of Latin America in what reminds the observer of a potential stranglehold.

In these slums are found the most severe symptoms of social disorganization, as families tend to break up, jobless adults scrounge for scraps to build a shack, and literally thousands of persons suffer from hunger and malnutrition. Among these unfortunate people can be found agitators for a variety of causes and ideologies, and they frequently find a receptive audience. It is among the hundreds of thousands of these urban slum dwellers that the connection between hunger and revolution may be found.

Revolution in Latin America

Real revolution in Latin America has been a rarity. However, illegal changes of government have certainly taken place with disconcerting regularity. The small nation of Honduras, for example, has experienced 136 *coups d' etat* in 147 years of independence from Spain, and only two constitutionally elected chiefs of state have completed their terms. Honduras remains a good example of the effect of the traditional social structure in which a small, wealthy elite dominates the majority of the population which is poor, hungry, and precariously educated. Pressures are building up all over Latin America as the frustrated victims of the social, economic, and political injustices begin to believe that they may be able to do something about it.

Much of the momentum of the coming explosion in Latin America erupts from the masses in the urban slums surrounding every major city. Crime, vice, and hunger are common in such slums, but the inhabitants soon learn their importance as potential voters. In election campaigns these squatters become important factors in political calculations. By practical experience, slum dwellers come to realize their potential power in electoral years. Agents and representatives of various political and ideological persuasions seek to win the support of these persons. The grinding poverty, and the painful awareness of the proximity of affluence which such "sub-Americans" experience, can assist in transforming unemployed, hungry people into a potentially rebellious mass.

As an increasing number of such persons become literate, often by attending night classes after moving to the city, or through the activity of "peasant leagues" in certain rural areas, an awareness of the possibilities for a better way of life increases. Transistor radios can now be found even in remote corners of the Amazon basin, or in the Andes mountains; they bring a new message to millions. This message has a constant refrain. "Life can be better; the old order must change; people don't have to be hungry, illiterate, or jobless." Promises are being made to the poor of the earth which, to fulfill them, will require a discarding of old systems. As one travels through Latin America today, he is impressed with the assurance with which people talk of the coming revolution.

Only three countries in Latin America have experienced a thoroughgoing social revolution during this century—Mexico, Bolivia, and Cuba. All of these have been accomplished by violence and bloodshed. As a result, many persons who are seeking radical changes in the social and economic structures are convinced that such innovation will come only through violent means. The power elite, they argue, will not give up their privileges without a fight.

Revolution Is Inevitable

Without doubt revolution is coming in Latin America. Its causes are rooted in the deep injustices of the traditional social structure. With increasing urbanization and industrialization, the focus of power is shifting away from the traditional "lords of the manor" to commercial and industrial leaders. The rising demands of an awakening lower class, and increasing "middle sectors" of the social structure, will force change to come. Increasing thousands are being convinced that it is not God's will that they remain poor; they now believe it is the result of the exploitation of the poor by the rich and powerful. The old structures of privilege and prestige based on family ties and control of cheap labor will have to change.

The effect of the presence of Americans—businessmen, governmental representatives, teachers, and missionaries—probably is a greater factor in encouraging change than is communist influence.

47

Certainly communists did not create the situations of elite dominance which produced poverty, hunger, and despair. These are the ingredients of which revolutions are made, and they exist in increasing proportions in Latin America. The ironic part of the present revolutionary expectancy is that North Americans have helped to produce it. Through programs of sanitation and literacy, films in theaters and on TV, advertising of American products by all possible means, and the preaching of an individualistic, progress-oriented gospel, North Americans have stimulated Latin Americans to desire the freedoms and the material possessions hitherto unavailable to them.

Without a doubt we can conclude that numerous factors within the traditional social structure, plus the effect of outside influences—democratic and communistic—are bringing much of Latin America to the takeoff stage for radical socioeconomic and political change. The urgency of the situation is aggravated by the increasing despair felt by persons who have been convinced that life can be better, yet whose real income is dropping, and whose hunger is increasing. Few informed observers would disagree with John Gunther who, after his recent trip through South America, wrote: "This is indeed a continent on the brink of revolution. . . . A genuine prerevolutionary pattern has been reached. . . . People are so desperate for change and improvement that they will take almost anything."

The Role of the Church

In the face of the social, economic, political, and spiritual realities in Latin America, what is the role and responsibility of the church? Certainly the traditional structure and order demonstrates the basically selfish nature of man, the inhumanity of man to his fellows. The church must speak a prophetic message of judgment on the systems which have produced hunger, poverty, and despair in the hearts of the masses. Professor Richard Shaull writes: "The most important single fact in the revolution of our time is the presence in it of the Christian church as an evangelistic movement, proclaiming to all men the meaning of their own existence, and the possibilities of life which lie before them."

The increasingly urgent demands for change should find in us a sympathetic response. Christians must identify themselves as individuals and as members of the body of Christ with the "wretched of the earth." Mennonite churches should find it easy to empathize with Latin America's fever for change and for social justice. Our forefathers also had radical solutions for their society's ills. Surely we can identify ourselves with people who hope for enough to eat, sufficient clothing and housing, and most of all for the opportunity to be self-respecting persons. Our current middle-class status may have robbed some of us of concern for the poor and hungry in the land, but it is encouraging to hear what Mennonite Central Committee is doing in various parts of the world. Many of the projects indicate that some of us are redemptively radical.

A Divided Response

The church in Latin America is divided on its response to the challenge of radical social change with a spectrum as broad as that in the United States. At one extreme are those groups who insist that the church is to "save souls and stay out of politics." At the other extreme might be placed the ecumenical organization, Church and Society in Latin America (ISLA). ISLA is convinced that the church must ally herself with the revolutionary ideals of Latin-American nationalists.

As a result, a revolution appears to be brewing within Catholic and Protestant groups themselves. The polarization of positions, with one group calling for gradual, peaceful change and the other suggesting that violence may be necessary for real change to occur, would appear to be sharper with the passing of time. Perhaps both positions are two myths which oversimplify social and political reality.

One of the most significant developments since Vatican II has been an increasing interaction between Christians of all denominations. We find much common ground in our understanding that true faith will involve us in seeking to rectify the *causes* as well as the *consequences* of sociopolitical and economic injustice. Encounters between Catholics and Protestants are taking place at an ever-increasing pace, and numerous groups have stated clearly the church's responsibility to get at the root of the injustices through action in the marketplace as well as in the sanctuary.

Dr. Jose Miguez-Bonino told the Associated Mennonite Seminaries in April 1968 that "the struggle for justice is indeed the basic question in Latin America today." However, Professor Miguez noted that the church's role is similar to that of the parable. She must be organized and seek to act in ways appropriate to the body of Christ, while assuring that her structure and her actions may be translated into societal terms. Only in this way can the particularity and the relevance of the church be maintained.

Do the Deeds of Christ

The church serves needy men and women "in the name of Christ"—representatives of Christ in today's world. Certainly the Mennonite Central Committee's involvement in relief work, agricultural and community development projects, literacy and sanitation campaigns, and other programs which speak to the felt needs of our brethren, is part of the church's way of doing the deeds of Christ. I have been especially impressed with MCC's policy of cooperating with local Christian groups. Our cooperation with the Methodists in Bolivia, and the Evangelical Confederation of Brazil, shows Christian interaction at its best. This interdenominational cooperation is one of the important "deeds of Christ." It is a practical demonstration of Christian unity and brotherhood. MCC sets an excellent example for all our churches in its willingness to serve with others and not be concerned about who gets the credit. The Gurupi Project in northern Brazil, where MCC workers are cooperating with Christians of various evangelical denominations in a colonization program, is just one example of doing the deeds of Christ.

Show the Spirit of Christ

To demonstrate the spirit of Christ is to act in love and understanding. When our Lord began His ministry, He quoted the passage from Isaiah 61:1, 2: "The Spirit of the Lord is upon me, because he has anointed me to preach good news to the poor. He has sent me to proclaim release to the captives and recovering of sight to the blind, to set at liberty those who are oppressed, to proclaim the acceptable year of the Lord" (Luke 4:18, 19).

It is clear from this statement that one cannot separate so-called secular activities from the sacred ones. Ministering to the heart and the body of the neighbor is to show the spirit of the Lord. If the church expects to preach good news, to proclaim release, and to set at liberty, its representatives will be involved in many activities in Latin America. Surely we will not give medical assistance to poor people without also providing the necessary information and means for family planning. To do otherwise is to increase the long-term suffering of the poor and the hungry. It is not an act of love.

The church must accept its share of the blame for the current population explosion, for only recently have we been courageous enough to act on our better knowledge. To show the spirit of Christ will lead the church in Latin America to confront the issues of population pressures by participating in family planning programs; to take a stand against social and economic injustice by encouraging radical change in the structures of society; to indicate our disapproval of repressive regimes by not cooperating with them in the suppression of liberty and freedom. The church will stop eulogizing social order if it is bought at the high price of social injustice.

I am convinced that to show the spirit of Christ today is to see the hand of God in the coming revolution in Latin America. As followers of the Prince of Peace, we cannot condone violence. But the extent of violence in the revolutions in Latin America, as well as in the United States, is determined by those who currently hold power, and refuse to give up their positions of prestige and privilege in order to achieve a more equitable socioeconomic system. Christian values will determine that we may choose to suffer with the victims of repressive regimes, rather than utilize their praetorian peace to carry out a project which in itself would be perfectly proper.

To show the spirit of Christ today means more than providing food to the hungry. It will involve dealing with the causes of hunger. It will involve us in agricultural, educational, and political processes. For such a spirit, we may expect the world to hate us. It is a sign of progress to hear that Vietnam Christian Service personnel are not preferred passengers in American military vehicles. It will be a sign of progress when Mennonites stop praising Latin-American military regimes which stifle the liberty and expression of dissenters, even though they give special privileges to favored minorities.

We may need to be silent or circumspect with our criticisms of such governments, but surely we need not praise them. The church must verbalize its dismay with the current exploitation of the poor by the rich, and seek ways to bring about a peaceful revolution. In terms of a desire for justice, we are on the side of the revolutionaries; we hope that it may be a peaceful revolution. But if worse comes to worst, to show the spirit of Christ will cause us to suffer violence rather than seek to defend an unjust, though orderly, status quo.

Speak the Message of Christ

As the church seeks to identify with the needs and hurts of suffering peoples, she is drawn irresistibly to programs which will combat hunger and injustice. And just as surely as night follows day she will incur the displeasure and hatred of those who defend the traditional order. It becomes a temptation in such a situation to expend our best energy at the physical, political, and socioeconomic tasks which must indeed be performed. But surely if we do the deeds of Christ, and show the spirit of Christ, we must also share the gospel message of Christ. It is all part of one package.

Sin and selfishness are causes of the present human predicament. Man's alienation from God, and from his fellows, is the root cause of the problems we have been considering. Any Christian effort which neglects sharing the message of salvation is less than Christlike. It has never been clear to me how the church proclaims Christ without seeking to lead men and women to accept Him as Lord. To suppose that we have spoken the message simply by doing the deeds and showing the spirit of Christ, may become an excuse to avoid the specific witness which sharing the message of Christ implies.

The church's involvement in confronting human hunger and immanent change, as a corporate body, is a response to the biblical vision of unity among men. We seek to be brothers with all men. Such a vision counsels peacemaking, not violence. Violent revolution may indeed remove current oppressors, but other groupings sooner or later take their place and oppression continues. The church has the privilege of serving a hungry world whose needs are far greater than bread. We seek to share Jesus Christ and His Spirit; that response which provides love where hate has ruled, unity instead of dissension, joy for sorrow, and hope in place of despair. God's challenge is our goal, "Let justice roll down like waters, and righteousness like an ever-flowing stream" (Amos 5:24).

5/ BY ATLEE BEECHY

Peacemaking in Vietnam

The peacemaking task in Vietnam is difficult and complex. Many interacting forces within the country and many outside influences make the reconciling work both complicated and challenging. Part of the peacemaking must take place inside Vietnam, but an important dimension, perhaps the most significant, is that which must take place outside—in our homes, communities, churches, and in our national life.

Relief Work in Vietnam

The Mennonite Central Committee went to Vietnam in 1954 in response to the disorder and the needs of refugees arising out of the war and the division of the country. From 1954 to 1965 during a period of growing violence, suffering, and disorder, twenty-nine Mennonite Central Committee workers rendered medical and other services in what is now South Vietnam. Mennonite Central Committee personnel established and developed a relationship of mutual confidence with representatives of the 50,000 member Evangelical Church of Vietnam and were well received by the Vietnamese people.

Vietnam Christian Service came into being early in 1966 as a result of growing concern of American Protestants for what was happening in Vietnam. Church World Service, the relief arm of some thirty Protestant groups in the National Council of Churches, and Lutheran World Relief, representing Lutheran groups not in the National Council, initiated a new cooperative relief program.

Vietnam Christian Service built on the strong and favorable reputation of the Mennonite Central Committee in Vietnam. At least two characteristics make the current program different from other relief efforts. The first of these is the nature of the cooperative relationships in Vietnam Christian Service. The memorandum of understanding covering these relationships is very simple. It brings together the resources of all three agencies but designates the Mennonite Central Committee to administer the total program. In addition, there are Vietnam field cooperative relationships between Vietnam Christian Service and the World Relief Commission, the relief arm of the National Association of Evangelicals, and with the Evangelical Church of Vietnam. The program is projected as a temporary arrangement and is to be reviewed annually.

In the second place, the Vietnam Christian Service program is being carried out in a country now at war. The people of Vietnam are caught in a tragic combination of historical, economic, geographic, military, and political factors, many of them beyond their own control. The desire for a national identity free from all foreign domination has deep historical, nationalistic, cultural, and psychological roots. Occupation, resistance, struggle for independence and for economic, social, and political reform are important concepts in understanding the history of these people. The Chinese occupied the country for almost a thousand years. The French came in the middle of the nineteenth century and remained in the country until 1954 with the exception of the World War II years. The Japanese occupied Vietnam during those years. The United States supported the Vietnamese struggle against the Japanese during World War II. Later the U.S. supported the French in their attempts to regain control of the country and since 1954 the United States has become increasingly more involved in the situation economically, politically, and militarily.

The pace of military activity has increased rapidly. In 1960 there were less than 1,000 Americans serving as advisers in Vietnam. Today the number of U.S. military personnel in Vietnam is over 525,000. This large-scale escalation of military activity has led to an upward leap in the number of refugees and to a proportionate escalation of suffering, dislocation, and despair. Surprise attacks and guerrilla terrorism, heavy bombing and artillery blasting describe certain dimensions of this terrifying activity. It is estimated that over half of the 15 million Vietnamese live in so-called contested or disputed areas. These are the geographic areas where fear and insecurity and self-preservation are the dominant motivating factors in the lives of the people. This real, although undeclared, war has created approximately two and a half million refugees in the past four years in South Vietnam alone. Half of these live in temporary camps and shelters. A small percent have been settled in new areas and a limited number have returned to their former villages and hamlets. Some of these have been forced from their homes two and three times. The plight of those not living in camps is equally serious, for many have moved into overcrowded hamlets, towns, and centers of population like Saigon. Saigon quadrupled its population since World War II and is today the most crowded city in the world.

There are deep emotional and spiritual needs arising out of this cultural and geographic disruption and dislocation. The nice-sounding social, economic, and political goals often seem far away for those who suffer most from the war. An American soldier said recently, "The villagers remember better those who drop the bombs than they do those who put on the bandages." All these factors combine to create a sense of bewilderment and disconnectedness among the Vietnamese. This may express itself in idleness, in vacant withdrawal, or in overt hostility.

Vietnam Christian Service

Vietnam Christian Service is seeking to carry out a ministry of compassion in spite of many problems and complexities. There are problems of transportation and communication, of earning the confidence and trust of the people, of a penetrating war mentality and a military dictatorship, of red tape, of housing, of soaring prices and a disrupted economy, of corruption, of war weariness and a mood of despair, and of a breakdown of moral, social, and legal standards. In the midst of these there also is the problem or opportunity of establishing and maintaining identity as a Christian-motivated and church-sponsored witness.

The objectives of Vietnam Christian Service include the following: the development of an efficient relief ministry, the strengthening of the Christian presence, and the bearing witness to the power of reconciling love. Are these objectives being achieved? It is too early to give a measured evaluation but some preliminary comments can be made. In the first place, the planned, enlarged program of relief activities has come into being and appears to be functioning satisfactorily in spite of many difficulties.

Second, the degree to which the program has brought the Christian presence into the midst of the disorder of Vietnam and has enlarged and strengthened the church is difficult to fully measure. It would appear that in the areas where our personnel have been working for a period of time, the Vietnamese recognize our workers as representing the church, and as different from the rest of the Western power structure. Identification of our workers, our centers, and our vehicles is helping to establish this image. Our personnel do not live behind barbed wire, or in barricaded and guarded quarters. The international character of our team is helping to make visible the international character of the church.

The program is largely service-centered; therefore, competent and dedicated personnel are absolutely essential. The church sponsorship of the program is crucially important and this requires clear identity with the Vietnamese people in their suffering. The situation also demands a definite witness to the universal, caring nature of the church.

The third objective is related to making a witness to the reconciling power of love in the midst of hate and violence. The basis of our peace position and our desire to help all the needy Vietnamese regardless of political affiliation has been presented to various church groups in Vietnam. It also has been personally interpreted to the U.S. ambassador to Vietnam and to high-ranking U.S. military and AID officials there. The question, "Why are you here?" has come to relief workers hundreds of times from refugees, other Vietnamese, and American civilians and military personnel. Contacts with Vietnamese government officials also offered opportunity for interpreting our position. The Mennonite missionaries spoke pointedly to the peace question in their widely publicized 1967 Christmas letter. A Vietnam Peace Advisory Committee and consultations and visits by MCC Peace Section members have been additional resources for peacemaking. Letters of concern about the war have been sent to President Johnson four times since 1965 by the Mennonite Central Committee, and other presentations have been made to governmental and other leaders by various individuals and groups.

Should the Church Be in Vietnam?

In light of this picture does the Mennonite Church belong in Vietnam? The church does have a responsibility for being at work amidst the suffering and dislocated people of the country. We have a responsibility to be a channel of God's concern for these people. In addition, as long as we can effectively work and maintain a defined Christian witness which is not an embarrassment to the Vietnamese or a danger to them, it is imperative that the church do everything possible to end this terrible violence and suffering and to shift the conflict to the conference table, and to influence public policy in that direction. Not everyone will agree that the church should be involved in both of these areas. There will be differences about the degree and method of involvement. Such differences should be recognized and discussed in a spirit of Christian mutual respect. Some may want to work for an ending of the war only through prayer, others through interviews and discussions, others through letters and articles which focus upon clarifying and questioning the assumptions and policies of the governments involved. Some people also tend to feel that we have an important responsibility to work at longer range reconciliation and rebuilding tasks whenever and wherever found.

There are four reasons why the peacemaking mission of the Mennonite Church in Vietnam remains important.

1. There continues to be great suffering and human need in this country. People are being destroyed—burned and bombed, and ambushed and tortured. Family and community structures have been fractured through long years of violence and war and by a massive military presence. Christians have been commissioned, commanded, to be the compassionate community, to be love in action, to minister the cup of cold water "in the name of Christ," and to stand beside the dislocated, disinherited, disrupted, and despairing. In one sense, we are to become the channel whereby some measure of hope and meaning may be restored, "to bind up the wounds and to rebuild the old waste places." I believe we must be there if we are true to the mission of the church as it is found in the New Testament. Donald Miller says, "The church is the body of Christ expressing Christ's concern for the whole world and its mission is to be Christ's action in the world today." We must be in Vietnam even if no one responds to the message in any formal or direct way, even if we are not gratefully received, or even if we are misunderstood and hated!

2. I think we belong in Vietnam because of the great general disruption, tension, and conflict in that country. There is a tremendous power struggle within the country, there is the shattering impact of the Western presence, there is an accumulation of despair, there is serious economic dislocation, and there is tremendous social and moral disruption. It would seem as if we have a high responsibility and a genuine obligation to be the Christian presence in the midst of all of this. To work toward reconciliation and peacemaking would seem to involve such a commitment.

3. Vietnam symbolizes the military mentality and the military dominance of part of the Western world. It not only symbolizes this in Vietnam, but is the actual place where violence and the sword are at work and where the resulting forces of hate and fear become real in the lives of the people. Behind all of this there is the struggle of the Vietnamese people to recover a measure of self-respect, to find their own national identity, and to achieve their own national aspirations. Vietnam is a pivotal spot in the growing military domination in our world. I believe the church must be

present to witness to the way of suffering love in this situation.

A considerable part of a small city was destroyed during the February 1968 Tet offensive by Vietcong activity, the massive U.S. bombing response, military ground action by the North Vietnamese and the Saigon government troops. In the midst of this situation a VNCS worker rallied the students and together they started to clean up the rubble and to rebuild. Commenting on this experience he said, "I feel that I am able to leave a witness to the bridge-building power of the God of love."

4. There is considerable diversity of religious life and activity in Vietnam and there is need and opportunity for interaction and witness among the groups who are seriously trying to strengthen the Christian church there. This ought to be done with great humility and with great sensitivity and understanding. If it is done in this way, we will surely be enlarged and enriched through the experience.

We have a unique opportunity to help build understanding between these varied groups and to be a witness and demonstration that the church is international in character and transcends national boundaries; that the Great Commission means a strong evangelical outreach, the proclamation of the prophetic word against evil wherever found, and an expression of compassionate concern for the total needs of man, and that the message of love and reconciliation lies at the heart of the gospel.

These days provide opportunity to witness to many who have not heard the good news and to speak to a large variety of Christian groups. We must seek the Spirit's guidance as we move further into this witness. There are, of course, risks involved but I wonder if we should be unduly concerned about such risks. But perhaps we should be most concerned about our obligations as affluent Christians in this moment in history.

Periodic efforts have been made to open relief work in North Vietnam and in areas under the control of the National Liberation Front. Some clothing and medical supplies were sent to North Vietnam in late 1966 and early in 1967. Applications for exploratory visits and some interpretative talks have taken place at several places.

Attempt at Christian Diplomacy

Mennonites have been uneasy about their inability to more clearly define their peace concerns and to more fully implement their basic relief principles in regard to these two areas. During the summer of 1968, at the request of the Mennonite Central Committee, I spent five weeks contacting representatives of the National Liberation Front and the Democratic Republic of Vietnam in Europe and Southeast Asia. In these conferences we discussed Mennonites and their beliefs, our historic peace position and our concerns for peace in the current situation, our relief history, philosophy, and our current relief program. We expressed concern for the suffering and dislocation caused by the war, what the Mennonites are saying about it, and finally explored possible relief projects for the people in these areas. The time seemed appropriate to make these contacts. I was courteously and respectfully received.

Some understanding of the basis for our position and how our position differs from other peace groups was evident. Appreciation for our concerns and our readiness to help their people was repeatedly expressed. I believe these contacts will help build relationships which may lead to Mennonites becoming involved in relief work in these additional areas. Even if it should not result in this development, I believe it urgent that we continue to register our concerns with DRVN and NLF representatives. Our faith demands such a response; in addition we must follow this course for the sake of our own spiritual health.

Vietnam and American Christians

There are certain additional factors related to our Vietnam peace witness which also need to be examined. Do we not have to admit that our complete intervention into the life of the people of Vietnam, the growing take-over and control of all facets of their life, and our growing destruction of the country to advance, at least in part, our own foreign policy and our own national interest, is wrong? I take the same position in regard to China and

Russia's insertion into the affairs of Vietnam, even though that involvement to date is less than is our own United States involvement. Does any country or combination of countries have the right to risk the lives of millions of people in an exploding military activity? The U.S. support of a military dictatorship and a privileged class government which is either unable or unwilling to bring about needed social and economic reforms is an important part of the moral aspect of the total situation. The use of massive amounts of human and natural resources and power for destructive purposes in light of the immense needs of Southeast Asia and the world is totally wrong and cannot but bring divine retribution and judgment upon us for such misuse of power and resources. In this situation the church must continue to proclaim the good news with vigor and imagination and utter the prophetic word of judgment against war and violence. Such a word must be given in a spirit consistent with the message of reconciliation.

What obligations do these convictions place upon us? If it is not possible to sit in comfortable affluence nor rest in cozy self-righteousness, some positive action is necessary. First, we need to pray with enlarged understanding and intensity. This means more than saying "bless the poor people in Vietnam." This requires confession of the sins of our church and nation, and praying for government representatives of all nations involved, for the 2,500,000 refugees in South Vietnam, for unknown numbers of refugees in North Vietnam, for all who suffer because of the war, for the Christians and non-Christians in Vietnam, and for the missionaries and relief workers.

Second, it is necessary to be informed about this complex situation to the greatest degree possible and join my fellow Christians in prayer, in study and discussion, in clarifying position, and in planning action steps. It is urgent to come to a position with conviction. We cannot assign to government responsibility for decision-making in issues which have moral and ethical aspects.

Third, it will be natural to discuss the issues and questions with neighbors and fellow workers within the context of our understanding of the biblical message and the Vietnam situation.

With these convictions, we can select and cooperate with those whose efforts are to move the Vietnam conflict to the conference table.

We should register our Christian concern to representatives of government through prayers, letters, conferences, and other means of communication. We need to support those lonely men in public office who seek to end the war in Vietnam now, who say we must allocate larger amounts of resources to find such a way, and who ask our government to intensify its negotiating efforts.

The nonresistant Christian cannot be indifferent or complacent or ignore the moral dimensions of this conflict. He must find effective and consistent ways to affirm his faith and to protest against the evil of this day. The opportunities for peacemaking are immense. The Mennonite Church is at work in the hamlets and in the teeming cities across the world. The pastor of a large Lutheran church in Berlin told me, "I believe the only authentic voice in Protestantism today is the voice of the historic peace churches." This is a sobering reflection and if he is at least partially right, then the coming days must be viewed with humility, expectant faith, enlarged commitment, and a new sense of urgency. God forgive us if our concern for peace fails to move across this country and the world to those millions of people caught in the wheels of poverty, fear, hate, and violence.

II

VOICES OF FAITH

6/ BY RICHARD C. DETWEILER

Peace Is the Will of God

The Scriptures provide a theology for peacemaking based on four assertions: that peace is the will of God for man; that God's peace action has taken place in Jesus Christ; that Christians are called to be God's ministers of reconciliation; that God's action in Christ forms the basis and pattern for Christian peacemaking.

Peace Is the Will of God for Man

This premise is our rock-bottom starting point. If peace is God's will, and strife or brokenness of life in any form reflects the sin of man, we have a powerful thrust and motivation toward peacemaking. We do not begin by talking about whether the war in Vietnam is justified or not, or about the relative merits of protest marches as peace action. We begin with the revelation that God's past, present, and future will for man as shown by the Scriptures is peace. Apart from revelation we have only a relative basis for peacemaking which may change with historical circumstances of time and place.

It seems hard to discover in the Old Testament that peace is the will of God, for these Scriptures are largely a record of human conflict, and at times God seems to lend sanction to it. Nevertheless, the Old Testament provides some understandings that lay groundwork for Christian peace action. For even here human strife and broken relationships in any form are considered the result of man's sin.

Genesis 1 and 2 show God's intended state for man. Genesis 3 and 4 record how man in his self-will and move toward independence fell into disharmony with God, with himself, with his environment, and his family, and his fellowmen. Human conflict, including war, must be seen in the context of man's separation from God, not as God's intention. Mennonite interpretation of the Scriptures has historically held that human strife always has been viewed within the category of man's sinful action.

God orders and overrules and works through man's sinful ways to accomplish His will, but that is very different from saying, for example, that war is God's will. Man's sinful acts are attributable to his own state and its consequences, not to God's intention.

God's will for man's redeemed life is forecast in the Old Testament. The Ten Commandments are God's revelation of His moral law and show the divine mind with regard to man's conduct in all relationships. The last six commandments reflect God's will for human relations. Exodus 20:12-17. There is no sanctioning of conduct that represents or engenders strife.

King David was given his military victories by God's power. Yet he was not allowed to build the temple, for God said: "You have shed much blood and have waged great wars; you shall not build a house to my name, because you have shed so much blood before me upon the earth" (1 Chronicles 22:8; 28:3). This provides a glimpse of God's intent and will in the midst of Israel's success in war against pagan powers.

Throughout the messages of the Old Testament prophets, it becomes progressively clear that the state of life existing even among God's own people was not what God yet intended to bring about and that He would establish a new covenant of peace. Jeremiah 31:31-34; Ezekiel 37:26. The prophetic vision reveals that the days of warfare for God's people are over, and the dawn of a new nature of life is at hand.

These forecasts also indicate that the God-intended life of peace will be brought about by the reign of Christ and man's being given a new nature whereby he can live in right relation with God and his fellowmen. Ezekiel 11:19, 20; Isaiah 9:6, 7.

The Old Testament meaning of salvation is closely linked with the meaning of peace. Peace is not considered a fringe benefit of salvation, but salvation itself is seen as the restoration of harmony of life. Peace and salvation are viewed in terms of deliverance from estrangement, fear, conflict, oppression, and injustice. Salvation is peace, a state of security, the result of God's action to restore right relations and a right state of life.

The Old Testament word for "peace," *Shalom*, means "completeness," and indicates that peace has to do with the total welfare of persons, not only with an inner state of feelings in the heart or peace of mind. In fact, the Old Testament seldom associates the term "peace" directly with inner feelings, but rather with one's relationships and state of life.

Not only is righteousness regarded as an attribute of inner being, but it is viewed as right action toward others. God shows forth His righteousness by His right acts toward men and men are called to participate in God's right actions. The ideal state is when peace and righteousness kiss each other. Psalm 85:10. The effect of right actions is peace. Isaiah 32:16. The prophet Jeremiah criticizes the cry, "Peace, peace," as false when it covers over lightly the "wound [hurts] of my people" (Jeremiah 5:28; 6:13, 14).

In the Old Testament, peace is viewed in terms of this life. The Old Testament has a vague awareness of the hereafter, but the expectation of a new state of life is oriented to a future on earth. The people of God expected Him to act in their historical existence in the world to bring about salvation, righteousness, and peace. Isaiah 55:12, 13.

Finally, the Old Testament is rightly interpreted through God's revelation in Christ as recorded in the New Testament. If the seeming ambiguities of the Old Testament (for example, God's command to destroy enemies vs. His denial of temple-building to David) leave any doubts that God's will is peace, the sacrifice of His Son for man's reconciliation as witnessed to by the New Testament is the conclusive revelation of His will.

We do not have a "flat" Bible. The Old Testament is as inspired as the New, but it is not equally revelatory of God's will in its fullness, for it is ultimately the Son who has been with the Father that "declares" God. John 1; Hebrews 1.

God's Peace Action Has Taken Place in Christ

"God was in Christ reconciling the world to himself, not counting their trespasses against them . . ." (2 Corinthians 5:19a). To reconcile means literally "to exchange." In Christ, God acted to exchange man's state of disharmony for one of peace. God's peace action has established the ground for man's restoration to Himself and the God-intended harmony of life.

To effect reconciliation, God in Christ took on the form of our life. Philippians 2:5-8. The meaning of the incarnation is that Christ entered into our human life in order to live it out for us, including tasting death for us, in a way that we ourselves as Adam's race failed to do. Peace for man has been wrought out in the world of man's actual existence. We are called not only to enter the death of Christ for us but to live in His life. That was the crucial difference in emphasis between the sixteenth-century Anabaptists and other major reformers. Anabaptists conceived of Christ not only as the Word of justification and acceptance with God, but as the Word of life. We say, therefore, that redemption or reconciliation is not simply a relief measure for man's soul, but a transformation of life. The new birth is not a rebirth of soul, but a rebirth of life. Christian peace action is based on the New Testament concept that salvation means not only the saving of soul, but the redeeming of life to its true state. 2 Corinthians 5:17.

To effect reconciliation, God in Christ dealt with sin as the cause of and the barrier to man's peace. "For our sake he made him to be sin who knew no sin, so that in him we might become the righteousness of God" (2 Corinthians 5:21). "By his wounds you have been healed" (1 Peter 2:24b). Reconciliation cannot be viewed apart from the cross. It is only in Christ that the hostility and enmity of man toward God and fellowmen has been broken down. Ephesians 2:14-18. Christian peacemaking can never circumvent the question of sin and forgiveness through Christ as the basic issue of reconciliation.

To effect reconciliation, God in Christ defeated the powers of Satan, sin, and death that hold man in bondage. Colossians 2:15. By the resurrection of Christ, a new order of life has been opened for man. A new kingdom has been established for him to enter. New relationships with God and his fellowmen have been made possible. A new nature of life is offered for man to partake of. Although our final redemption is yet to come, it has already been completed in Christ and in Him we are no longer subject to the powers of this present age. Our peacemaking is undergirded by the conviction that the powers that hold man from his God-intended life have been broken and that Christ is Lord. His reign is being established and will prevail forevermore. The power of the Holy Spirit is at work to bring to pass the divine will among men. Peacemaking is taking part in the reign of Christ.

To effect reconciliation, God in Christ has created a new body, a new humanity, a new community where the new life in Christ is shared and lived, where God's intention for man is being fulfilled. 1 Peter 2:9, 10. Christian peace action recognizes not only that peace is an individual matter between each man and God, but that God's purpose in reconciliation is to bring into being a people, a brotherhood, the church, wherein God's will for peace is demonstrated. Christian peacemaking is the task not only of individuals but of the church. The goal is not each man's peace of mind, but a new state of life together.

We Are Called to Be God's Ministers of Reconciliation

God has entrusted to Christians the ministry of reconciliation. 2 Corinthians 5:19, 20. This is a threefold ministry focusing on preaching (*kerygma*), service (*diakonia*), and living in the fellowship of the church (*koinonia*).

Christians are to carry the message that God has acted for us in Christ. This is called the kerygmatic function of the church, the proclamation of the good news, the witness by word of mouth that we have been reconciled to God and are called to accept God's forgiveness by acknowledging faith in the death and resurrection of Jesus Christ.

Peacemaking is saying to men, "We beseech you on behalf of Christ, be reconciled to God" (2 Corinthians 5:20). In one sense, we cannot make peace. Primarily we witness to the reality that we have been reconciled in Christ and call men to accept the peace that has been accomplished for them. Our witness is to point to the sacrifice of Christ, His victory over the powers of this age, His lordship and judgment over all things, and His coming again.

Proclamation must be joined with the ministry of deeds that brings healing to persons and makes their lives whole. The ministry of the word of reconciliation must be accompanied by reconciling actions. The love of God is not communicated by saying, "Be warm and fed." The ministry of reconciliation is that of healing the brokenhearted, bringing sight to the blind, giving liberty to them that are bruised, caring for the sick, relieving the oppressed, giving the cup of cold water in the name of Christ. Luke 3:18; Matthew 25:34-46; 1 John 3:16-18.

The church is called to peace action by "saying," "doing," and also by "being." The church is the community of forgiveness, the fellowship of healing. As the church makes visible in her life the reality of reconciliation, she becomes a healing force in society. Philippians 2:1-16; Ephesians 5:22-32. The church as the true church is the community of reconciliation where there is neither Jew nor Greek, bond nor free, high nor low, where barriers are broken down and the kingdom of Christ is made visible.

In summary, then, the church carries on her ministry of reconciliation by witnessing through word and deed to God's reconciling action in Christ, and by becoming in herself the hospital of healing for the brokenness of mankind.

God's Peace Action in Christ Forms the Basis and Pattern

for Christian Peacemaking

From this understanding of the biblical message for Christian peace action, we propose the following principles or elements of peacemaking:

(1) Christian peace action must be pointed toward the problem of man's broken relation with God and must be based on the principle of forgiveness. For example, the question of whether or not demonstrations such as protest marches are to be regarded as Christian peace action must be decided at least partly on whether such action is based primarily on the power of coercion or on the power of forgiveness. This is not to overlook the biblical perspective that conflict through the exposure of sin may often precede reconciliation.

(2) Christian peace action demands involvement where the brokenness of life calls for healing. As it is said, peace is not effected by someone broadcasting from a second-story window. At whatever point the unity of word and deed is lost, the attempt to minister reconciliation will fail. Reconciliation seen only in terms of man's soul will not be effective in redeeming man's life.

(3) Christian peace action must be consistent with the nature of God's peace action for man as revealed in the cross. To preach a gospel of reconciliation while at the same time supporting or even participating in military action as the will of God is the height of contradiction. The same must be said with regard to the Christian's attitude toward other social evils. Whenever the means by which we witness is inconsistent with the way of the cross we profess to follow, we are contradicting our message.

(4) Christian peace action will require suffering on our part. It will mean a dying to ourselves, for it will conflict with the spirit and patterns of the world and often bring on the hostility of the world. Jesus made this clear by His own experience and His teachings.

(5) Christian peace action will be directed not only to the "weaknesses" of society, but to the strongholds of society that carry responsibility for the sufferings of the weak. Both Jesus and the early church confronted the power structures of their time—the economic power structures, the social power structures, civil governing powers, and religious power structures, and called them to recognize the lordship of Christ and His judgments. Peacemaking involves a witness to the victory of Christ over every power that

holds man in bondage and calls all men to recognize their need of repentance. It should also be noted that the New Testament witness to power structures is person-centered.

(6) Christian peace action is based not on humanitarianism, but on the conviction that a new life for man has been opened by Christ's resurrection and that man can receive a new nature by which he is able to live in a new order of life free from the spirit of the world.

(7) Christian peace action recognizes that the Holy Spirit is acting in the world, convicting of sin, of righteousness (right actions), and judgment, and that peacemaking is cooperating with the power of God that is acting on the hearts and minds of men.

(8) Christian peace action realizes that the perfect state of man will not be fully achieved in this age, but that nevertheless the kingdom of Christ has been inaugurated and is moving toward its culmination in the coming of Christ when all things shall be put under His feet and the plan of God for man's peace shall be completed in full.

All Scripture quotations are taken from the Revised Standard Version.

7 /   BY SANFORD G. SHETLER

God's Sons are Peacemakers

Peace and war are not novel twentieth-century problems but ones which have plagued mankind since the beginning of time. Peace and war have, likewise, perplexed Christendom during its long history. The Reformation unfortunately did more to confuse the issue than to resolve it, and the church today inherits this legacy.

What the attitude should be of those who sincerely seek to do God's will is a matter of grave concern. Today there seems to be such a complexity of forces playing on the church that the whole issue has become even more complicated. To keep one's perspective clear and aligned with the Bible in such a circumstance is not easy. Mennonites, with their long peace tradition, should have something to say to our civilization on the question of peace and war. But just how this should be said and to whom is difficult to know. But regardless of the varieties of opinion on methods of "witnessing" to society on peace, we should not, above all, be caught fighting on how to preserve peace! Yet, at the same time, we should not become so readily absorbed with the ideas of individuals and organizations which bear only a faint resemblance to the biblical teaching on peace and nonresistance. A growing concern, too, on the part of many churchmen is the need of maintaining a rigorous teaching program on peace, lest in time of crisis our young men repeat the poor record of World War II in respect to taking the conscientious objector position. It is important, then, to review the biblical background on peace and war to derive the pattern for God's sons as true peacemakers.

In the Bible, Satan is portrayed as the instigator of brokenness in the world. One may, in a very true sense, say, "This is my Father's world," but it is also correct to say that the world is under the dominion of the usurper Satan. Thus, while it is not incorrect to say that God is at work in His world, much that transpires in our world today is, as someone has stated, "the maneuvering of Satan."

Satan is depicted in the Scriptures as one who constantly attempts to set man at variance with God, set God at variance with man, and set man at variance with man. In Genesis the devil, in the form of a serpent, to use the respected historic interpretation, said to Adam, "Yea, hath God said?" attempting to set man at variance with God. In the Book of Job, Satan is shown appearing before God to bring reproach on man: "Doth Job fear God for nought?" The Book of Revelation depicts Satan in this same role as the "accuser of . . . [the] brethren." "The accuser of our brethren is cast down, which accused them before our God day and night" (Revelation 12:10). In James 4 man is shown lusting and warring against man for selfish ends. Paul reminds us that we are "not ignorant of his [Satan's] devices" (2 Corinthians 2:11).

In addition, man is also frequently torn by internal frustration and conflicts, with the flesh and spirit being at war with each other. Obviously Satan often takes advantage of this internal turmoil. The first war was in heaven between Satan and God. Though set in an eschatological frame, Revelation 12:7 sheds light on this war of pre-history:

> Now war arose in heaven . . . and the dragon and his angels fought, but they were defeated and there was no longer any place for them in heaven. And the great dragon was thrown down, that ancient serpent, who is called the Devil and Satan, the deceiver of the whole world—he was thrown down to the earth, and his angels were thrown down with him.
> (RSV)

In Matthew 13:18-20 Satan is shown also as the great deceiver, the one who sows tares among the wheat. Matthew 4:8 portrays him as usurping authority over the nations as he offers Christ "all the kingdoms of the world." But Jesus would not accept this spurious short-circuiting of God's program, knowing that at the proper time in the plan of the Eternal, Jesus would indeed assume the title as Lord of the nations.

To summarize, the root of all human disorder and brokenness in the world is Satan himself, the archenemy of our souls. He is out to create chaos and destruction, to set men at variance with each other and with God. Men and nations are his tools, and not until all enemies are put under Christ's feet and Satan is bound will there be peace on earth.

How Peace Is Established

True peace among men can be established only when peace is first established in men's hearts and man is reconciled to God. "For in him all the fulness of God was pleased to dwell, and through him to reconcile to himself all things, whether on earth or in heaven, making peace by the blood of his cross" (Colossians 1:19, 20, RSV). Clearly Jesus is portrayed as the Great Reconciler, who, as man and God, can bridge the gap as no one else possibly could. Yet to man is assigned the supreme task of being the agent in this reconciliation process.

> All this is from God, who through Christ reconciled us to himself and gave us the ministry of reconciliation; that is, God was in Christ reconciling the world to himself. . . . So we are ambassadors for Christ, God making his appeal through us. We beseech you on behalf of Christ, be reconciled to God.

Today in many Christian circles the humanistic phase of *Shalom* (peace) has become the gospel, with the divine dimension being almost forgotten. But, as stated, there can be no peace among men so long as men are not first reconciled to God and are at peace with Him. This automatically places the priority in witnessing on

77

reconciling men to God and not on the establishment of a kind of artificial world peace among unregenerate men.

The Record of Man's Peacemaking Efforts

A quick review of man's peacemaking efforts in the past century and a half reveals the utter futility of the kind of peacemaking that deals only on the horizontal level—of trying to establish peace among men who have never been reconciled to God. Admittedly there have been some temporary successes along the way in settling national and international disputes through arbitration, which we do not wish to minimize. One notes the efforts of such organizations and institutions as the Hague Peace Tribunal, the World Court, the League of Nations, and the United Nations. This is not to mention the efforts of private individuals and organizations such as Henry Ford's peace ship during World War I, Buchman's "Moral Rearmament Program," the work of the Fellowship of Reconciliation, the War Resisters' League, and others. Many individuals connected with these efforts have labored with unflagging zeal for a "just and durable peace" with the kind of fervor Paul refers to in another context as "[having] zeal . . . but not according to knowledge." The Bible is clear in its predictions that there will be wars and rumors of wars, that nation will rise up against nation until the end of time, and no human effort will change this inevitable course of history.

In the midst of man's vain attempts to bring about peace without first bringing men into a peace relationship with God, we have witnessed several world wars and numerous lesser wars and conflicts. The situation has been constantly worsening with the whole human race being threatened now with extinction. Man's efforts toward peace have been amply exploited, but God's method has not. If instead, the church could have, in any epoch of history, become fully convinced of its divine role as reconciler, there is no doubt but that the history of the human race would have been different.

Knowing the futility of expanding her efforts in behalf of bringing peace to nations by human manipulation—by political or social reform, through education or direct peacemaking efforts, the church that is doing God's will, will attempt to discover her true task and try to be faithful in it. In peacemaking there can be no "second-best" program that can claim God's blessing or that will give any promise of lasting fruits.

God's revealed message, universal for all peoples and all time, clearly defines the path which the church must follow. The basic course of action is charted in the "Constitution of the Kingdom" (Matthew 5—8). The Book of Acts gives us the pattern the early church followed and the Epistles, the fuller revelation. From these there seem to emerge three distinct roles or services which the church must fulfill in its peace mission.

First, as stated before, the members making up the body of Christ must be reconciled to God themselves, before they can presume to undertake the high task of peacemaking among men. Second, to be effective peacemakers, Christians must themselves be the real salt of the earth. In the broadest sense, no one can be a peacemaker who is not himself an example of peace, both as a Christian and as a citizen. Personal, family, church, and community conflicts must be resolved on their respective levels before Christians can begin to set the world in order. Many an effective witness has been lost through inconsistency within the church itself. In 1 Peter 2 and 4 and in Romans 12 we have a good summary of the kind of conduct that should characterize the people of God in their witness to the world:

Personal—"Beloved, I beseech you as aliens and exiles to abstain from the passions of the flesh that wage war against your soul" (1 Peter 2:11, RSV).

Church—"And above all things have fervent charity among yourselves" (1 Peter 4:8, KJV).

Community—"Maintain good conduct among the Gentiles, so that

79

in case they speak against you as wrongdoers, they may see your good deeds and glorify God on the day of visitation" (1 Peter 2:12), and "As much as lieth in you, live peaceably with all men" (Romans 12:18).

State—"Be subject . . . to every human institution [every ordinance, KJV], whether it be to . . . governors as sent by him to punish those who do wrong and to praise those who do right. For it is God's will that by doing right you should put to silence the ignorance of foolish men. Live as free men, yet without using your freedom as a pretext for evil; but live as servants of God. Honor all men. Love the brotherhood. Fear God. Honor the emperor" (1 Peter 2:13-17, RSV).

Third, Christians are to assume the high role of ambassadors for Christ. This diplomatic designation connotes the relationship of the people of God to their heavenly kingdom in which they are citizens and underscores the fact that they are aliens in this world. As ambassadors representing their King, Christians are to serve as "negotiators" in making peace among men in their relation to God. Idealistically, if the church were to make disciples of all nations with anything close to a point of saturation, there would virtually be no more wars. But short of this, the utter futility and complexity of ever reaching a just and durable peace by any other means becomes completely apparent.

These roles will be achieved first through the preaching of the gospel, the *kerygma*, as represented in apostolic announcement that Jesus is Lord. The great missionary psalm (67) seemingly predicting the one chief objective of the church speaks of making "thy way . . . known upon earth, thy saving health among all nations." Significantly, this psalm includes the gospel in its broadest aspects, using such terms as "health," "[judging] the people righteously," "the earth . . . [yielding] her increase." Health, social justice, and material prosperity are all regarded as concomitants of the gospel as people are brought into a peace relationship with God. This, of course, is an ideal that has never actually been reached. Instead of the fear and frustration that follows "apartness from God," which is the seeming mood of our time, the nations, as the psalm states, could, if they were obedient to God, "be glad and sing for joy," and God would indeed "bless us."

Christ's last Great Commission was to go abroad and make disciples of all nations. This became the imperative of the early church and with phenomenal expansion the first centuries witnessed the spread of Christianity, a growth unequaled in any period of later history. Under the impact of this penetration, the pagan Roman Empire crumbled and such common evils as infanticide, slavery, immorality, and social injustice were either greatly reduced or totally ended. The Epistles bear witness to the large place given to the preaching-proclaiming of the *kerygma*. As Christ becomes Savior and Lord of men, they in turn assume their new obedience as bond slaves, becoming the vehicles through which God's way may be made known upon earth. There will never be a substitute for the preaching of the Word and never a new strategy by which men may witness to lost humanity.

The message must always be accompanied with a ministry of good deeds. Faith without works is dead. We cannot say to a brother or sister who is "naked, and destitute of daily food," "Depart in peace, be ye warmed and filled." Humanity today is looking for more than sermonizing; it is looking for a proof of our concern.

Looking over the pages of history one discovers that the church has fulfilled this double role of preaching and engaging in social service. One is impressed, to look at one example, at the tremendous work of J. Hudson Taylor and the China Inland Mission— how that by 1914 there were 250,000 baptized members and a chain of charitable institutions, hospitals, nurses' and teachers' training schools, and an agricultural extension program to help to raise the economic status of China. It is an unfair indictment against the Christian church to say, in the modern cliche, "the church has failed." The church has not failed. But admittedly, it has stopped short of its potential. It is significant, however, that as the missionary fervor of the last century and the early twentieth century began to fade out, the clamor for social justice and human betterment began to increase. This switch of priorities betrays the changing role of the church.

Mennonites in this regard have had a good, though not a flattering, record. Our first foreign mission program began with a relief program to feed the starving people of India. Frank Laubach, known as the world's literacy expert, though interested in teaching the world to read through the teaching of portions of the Bible, is interested no less in social service. In this way he focuses on a happy blend of preaching and deeds of mercy. In a recent address noting the desperate need today in many countries, he warned, "If we do not heed the hand raised for help, that same hand will soon come up as a fist."

The Christian and War

In their role as peacemakers, God's sons can have no part in the war effort. Participation in war is a repudiation of all that Christianity represents. Matthew 5 conveys the teaching of the New Testament on the doctrine of peace:

> Do not take revenge on someone who does you wrong. If anyone slaps you on the right cheek, let him slap your left cheek too. And if someone takes you to court to sue you for your shirt, let him have your coat as well. (TEV) (See also John 18:36; Romans 12:19).

Noncombatant service in the army, which involves taking care of the wounded or keeping war supplies on hand or engaging in support operations of whatever kind, is still a necessary part of the war effort and at once implicates man in the whole process of taking human life. A consistent attitude on the war question will also rule out working in war industries and buying war bonds. For some, payment of taxes in support of war is considered unethical. Yet there seems to be no scriptural indication that such a distinction in the payment of taxes is necessarily warranted by the New Testament command to pay tribute.

Christians are not only commanded to refrain from fighting, but they must assume the positive role of being peacemakers. Jesus said, "Blessed are the peacemakers: for they shall be called the children of God" (Matthew 5:9). William Barclay makes the significant paraphrase, "The man who makes peace is engaged in the very work which the God of peace is doing." The Christian church has the unique obligation, because of its message of Christ-love, of being arbiters in the ministry of grace and healing in bringing men together who are at variance with God and man. To remain quiet rather than to cause trouble, a common alibi of those who avoid direct overtures toward peaceful settlements, is to shun the true role of peacemakers. Within the family of God, in the context of Romans 12, Galatians 6, and Matthew 18, we are to be "members one of another," bear each other's burdens, and restore those who err in a spirit of meekness. In the wider community Christians must live peaceably with all men, heap coals of fire on the heads of their enemies, and try to establish peace where there is brokenness. William Barclay speaks aptly of the "bliss bringing men together."

Social service that results in healing broken hearts, that restores wholeness by resolving inner conflicts, and through settling interpersonal difficulties, is Christian service of the highest order. Christianity cannot disregard men's whole nature and must constantly deal with total man in the total situation to effect any permanent results in peacemaking. The Hebrew word *Shalom* never means only the absence of trouble, but always everything which makes for man's highest good.

Conclusion

Finally, it should be noted that the church's task is performed largely through irradiation and not by legislation. The influence of the church as a totally committed witnessing body, will, by the very nature of its mission, "infiltrate" all sections and phases of society, including those persons and institutions which make up what we call the state. As the level of righteousness rises in a given society, the social ideals of that society will automatically rise. This is the Bible method referred to as irradiation, the process or quality of being the salt of the earth. We have seen, however, a trend that is disturbing, an attempt of the church to short-circuit this program by calling on men in the government who themselves are not necessarily reconciled to God, to effect social changes through legislation! Since the method of changing men's hearts through a redemptive ministry is considered the only proper method of the church, it becomes completely inappropriate to suddenly adopt a method that attempts through legislation to coerce men to be good.

Loudly and clearly the great appeal of the ages should be heralded today by the Christian church, "I beg of you in Christ's stead, be ye reconciled to God." This, and this alone, is the hope of the nations, the hope of every individual in achieving the highest good both here and hereafter. If only the church could presently awaken to its task of peacemaking in a society which is so greatly in need of reconciliation, what a change this would bring to our broken world!

8/ BY WILLARD SWARTLEY

Peacemakers: the Salt of the Earth

In the Sermon on the Mount (Matthew 5) Jesus describes the peacemaker as a son of God, then in verse 13 He also calls this same person or community of people to be the salt of the earth. The question thus emerges: How does the Christian peacemaker fulfill his call to be the salt of the society in which he lives?

This question provokes further questions. What is the peacemaker's style of life and action? What is the peace message and mission? How do God's people perform that mission? Does this mission include witness to political institutions about peaceful solutions to existing conflicts? By what methods, if any, do Christians speak to such institutions?

While it is difficult to directly answer these questions, there are, however, numerous biblical teachings which crucially guide us. In this discussion, therefore, we shall seek to understand these biblical teachings which form the bedrock and perspective of our answer to these questions. These teachings are: the meaning of the incarnation with a special discussion of atonement, the nature of the church, the biblical view of temporal government, and the biblical view of morality, including war.

Incarnation

When the Apostle Paul reflected upon the total meaning of Christ for the church and the world, he affirmed that the incarnation was meant to accomplish reconciliation both vertical and horizontal. In 2 Corinthians 5 Paul describes the incarnation and its purpose with these words, ". . . God was in Christ, reconciling the world unto himself. . . ." In Ephesians 2 Paul asserts that Christ having come in the flesh became our peace, thus breaking down all walls of hostility which separate men.

The blood of Christ, therefore, draws all men to the loving heart of God, thus enabling the creation of a new humanity in which both are made one. The incarnation culminates in atonement which is both vertically and horizontally an at-one-ment. God in Christ reconciles man to Himself and to one another.

The incarnate Christ's life and teachings provide us also a paradigm or blueprint for our own discipleship. We learn from Jesus the life of humble servanthood which does not despise but endures suffering. Philippians 2:5-11. Through the suffering of the cross, Jesus gained the crown. Numerous experiences and teachings of Jesus illustrate how Jesus' total life accorded with His Gethsemane and Calvary suffering, thus making peace by the blood of the cross.

While an analysis of Jesus' total life and teaching would be helpful, the following discussion focuses upon the temptations which exemplify His refusal to compromise the position of peace as God's way to Messiahship. Each of the three temptations in Matthew 4 and Luke 4 presents Jesus with a possible shortcut to Messiahship. While each temptation has personal appeal in the wilderness setting, yet each also has Messianic significance. Each temptation suggests a major compromise which Jesus faced in His earthly ministry.

In the first temptation Satan urged Jesus to satisfy His hunger by using His divine power to make bread out of stones. Undoubtedly this suggestion appealed directly to Jesus' hunger. But the temptation, as many Bible scholars explain, had also deeper significance. In this temptation Jesus wrestled with the whole issue of what kind of Messiah He would be. The possibility of becoming a popular king by miraculously providing bread for the multitudes became a live option in the life of Jesus. John 6. Hence Jesus could have become a kind of welfare Messiah. In a decisive way Jesus refused the temptation of material security. He has for men in every age given an example: "Man shall not live by bread alone, but by every word that proceeds from the mouth of God."

The second temptation confronted Jesus with the possibility of evading the cross by gaining popular Messianic support on a religious basis. The temptation is recorded in the form of an ancient prophetic expectation, namely, that when the Messiah comes He will suddenly appear in the temple area. Malachi 3:1. In one of the intertestamental books this expectation becomes even more specifically described. The Messiah when He comes will suddenly appear in the temple area by jumping off the temple roof. In light of this prophetic hope, Jesus was indeed struggling with this possible route to Messiahship. In Jesus' actual life the Palm Sunday entry into Jerusalem set the stage for possible religious, ecclesiastical Messiahship. Would Jesus now evade the cross, the way of love and peace, by following an alternative route to Messiahship?

Again Jesus was our example. He refused this temptation of becoming a popular, religious ecclesiastical leader by presuming upon His special powers of sonship and the applause of the crowd. His answer was, "You shall not tempt the Lord your God." Jesus heard clearly the call of obedience, the call to the cross, and He thus resisted any kind of ecclesiastical counterfeit. He was not about to become a pope or a bishop as an alternative to the clear call to a Messiahship rooted solely upon suffering love and atoning peace.

The third temptation confronted Jesus with a Messiahship of political power as an alternative to the cross. This temptation is especially crucial because whenever we discuss the question of peace, it is precisely the question of political power which must be dealt with. The temptation which Jesus faced was to bow down to Satan himself and through worship of Satan gain the kingdoms of this world. One might say that this is the temptation to gain earthly power by earthly means.

Now again as in the other temptations there comes a moment in Jesus' life when He struggles with such a possible evasion of the cross. In Gethsemane Jesus said He could call twelve legions of angels and by this power throw back the force of the Roman power. It seems as though Jesus as the Son of God had the prerogative to manifest His Messiahship on a political platform, but again Jesus did not submit to this temptation. He refused it. He in turn replied to Satan, "You shall worship the Lord your God and him only shall you serve."

With this final temptation Jesus resisted the alluring alternatives which confront men of every age. He resisted compromise on the basis of material power. He resisted compromise for ecclesiastical power. He resisted compromise for military power. These temptations clearly portray Jesus as one who chose absolutely and categorically the way of the cross, the way of suffering, peace, and reconciliation. Perhaps from this evidence more than any other we can observe how the peace position rests upon the bedrock level of the gospel.

Atonement

A second area to consider in understanding the meaning of Jesus lies in the cosmic significance of the atonement, resurrection, and exaltation. Repeatedly the New Testament speaks of Jesus' victory over all enemies. This emphasis is often called the Christus Victor view of the atonement. Jesus conquers all opposition.

The Gospels (Matthew 12:27-29; Luke 10:18) teach us that Jesus in His incarnation and ministry defeated and bound the powers of Satan. In Luke 10:18 Jesus says that as the disciples proclaimed the gospel and cast out the demons, he "saw Satan fall like lightning from heaven." Satan lost his ultimate power because the Messiah had come. In 1 Corinthians 15:26, 54-56 the Apostle Paul tells us that Jesus also vanquished the powers of death, thus defeating the last enemy and making Him Lord of all.

Jesus' victory over evil is manifest also in His conquest and defeat of all principalities and powers. The Apostle Paul affirms in Colossians 2:10 that Jesus is head over all principalities and powers. This point is crucially relevant for an understanding of our peace witness and responsibility. We will need to look later at what Paul means by principalities and powers. Suffice it to say at this point that these terms include the temporal governments and the affirmation is that Jesus is Lord over all these powers.

As this is a difficult point for us to understand, let us look more carefully at the New Testament teaching on this topic. The texts that must be examined are: Ephesians 1:20-23; Romans 8:35-39; Colossians 1:15-18; 2:10; 1 Corinthians 2:6-8; 15:20-28; 1 Peter 3:22. All of these emphasize that Jesus in His resurrection and exaltation has become Lord of all. He is head of everything. The picture in Ephesians is that Jesus is the head, the church is His body, and all powers outside those two realms are under the feet of Jesus. He is Lord over all. The church recognizes, knows, and confesses His lordship. The world denies it.

Because of Jesus' lordship over all men the atonement of Jesus has cosmic universal potential. The texts that describe this point are: Romans 8:18-25; Ephesians 1:10; Colossians 1:19, 20; Philippians 2:11: Revelation 5:13. These verses tell us that God's purpose in Jesus' life, death, resurrection, and exaltation is to ultimately unite all things in Christ. Thus, if the atonement has universal potential, we can never forget that all men are to be saved and that wherever war persists men are being killed who might be converted. Consequently, the very exercise of war militates directly against the possibility of fulfilling the Great Commission.

At this point we summarize our examination of the meaning of the incarnation for peace witnessing. The peace witness rests upon the example of Jesus who shows us the way of the cross by which we are reconciled both to God and to our fellowmen. Based upon the fact of cosmic atonement, the peace witness should be announcement, not advice; petition in the name of Christ, not only political counsel. In other words, something has happened in history to which our lives by both deed and word must bear witness. As peacemakers, our salting mission is to penetrate every realm of life and society with the fact and practical possibility of reconciliation, peace, and goodwill among men. We witness by life, deed, and word that hostility, conflict, and war are unnecessary and outright denials of the mission of Christ.

Church

The church is first and foremost an international, transcultural community. Galatians 3:28; Ephesians 2:11-22. As one body in Christ (Ephesians 4:1-16), the church, realizing that Christ's kingdom is ultimately not of this world (John 18:36), disowns all forms of nationalism. Committed and bound to an international brotherhood of Christian believers, the church always regards this allegiance more primary than any national loyalty or responsibility. Hence the church decisively confesses: "We ought to obey God rather than men." Because the church is an international brotherhood it considers participation in war a denial of its very universal, transnational nature. When one group of Christians takes up arms against another group of Christians, both groups deny their belief that Jesus and not Caesar is final Lord. They sacrifice Christian faith for national security.

This point is specifically noted by the early Anabaptist leader Michael Sattler in his discussion of the two orders of life to which the Christian is responsible. He refers to the one order as the order of sonship and the other order as the order of service. He uses the term "service" or "servant" to denote one who performs the duties and requirements of law. The servant lives on the level of legal mandate; the son, however, lives on the level of love and gospel ethic. Thus, the order of sonship transcends the order of legal service. The gospel transcends the law. Indeed, Sattler saw the law and temporal government as serving a legitimate function within God's total plan for history. But this is not the primary concern and purpose of God. That primary purpose is accomplished through the church, through the community of sons, and never should the community of sonship jeopardize or sacrifice its calling, its commitment, in order to carry forward a lesser legitimate function in the realm of law and government. Sattler distinguishes these two levels of obedience with the words "filial" and "servile." The son gives filial obedience whereas the servant renders servile obedience, obedience to law, which is always only a temporary order of life to sustain society so that the gospel might be preached and God's primary purpose for men accomplished. 1 Timothy 2:1-4.

This means then that our peace witness should be transnational if possible. In contemporary practical terms this means that the church should if possible give relief assistance to both North and South Vietnam. Our concern and commitment to the needs of men is universal regardless of the military zones which are in effect during times of war. Our statements of witness to temporal governments should be addressed to both sides of the conflict if this is possible.

Since many of our own leaders claim to be Christians, we have the additional responsibility to confront them with the sonship demands of the gospel and the servant demands of the law. They, of all men, should seek the best possible temporal order wherein justice and equity prevail. We have in our heritage the example of Menno Simons who again and again spoke forcefully to the magistrates regarding the way in which they could do their job better than the way they were doing it. By the word "better" I mean more in accord with the legal ethical norms of the Bible and therefore more humane.

The church as the church should act and speak on moral issues in contemporary society. Growing right out of the church's loyalty to the gospel the church must take a gospel stand regarding evils in the world, regarding war, regarding oppression of the poor, regarding inequality and injustice among men. The gospel does not annul the law. Instead, the gospel enables us to see the true intent and purpose of the law. Christians who understand the inner nuances of the law's voice, should of all men be on hand to leaven the formulation of human laws which ostensibly seek for norms of justice and equity among men.

Government

The passage in the New Testament to which we most often refer for a biblical understanding of government is Romans 13. This passage tells us that every authority or power that exists is ordained, instituted, or ordered of God (the Greek word used here has all three meanings). We can better understand this teaching if

91

we look more closely at the word "power." In the Greek, the word is *exousia*. This is the same word that is used again and again in the term "principalities and powers." The word "powers" in this term is the same Greek word as "power" in Romans 13.

A clue to understanding this term comes from a study of the Old Testament term "Lord of hosts." This phrase "Lord of hosts" is used repeatedly in the Old Testament literature. Psalms 89:5-9; 148:2; 102:21. The word "hosts" when it is translated from the Hebrew into the Greek Septuagint is translated by the Greek word *exousia* which is the same word which we have found in Romans 13 and in the New Testament term "principalities and powers." What does it mean then to talk about the Lord of the *exousia* in the Old Testament? The way to answer this question is to discover what the term *exousia* in the Old Testament means.

In Daniel 7:27 "hosts" or *exousia* designates temporal domains and governments. But the word "hosts" or *exousia* is also much more broadly used. In Psalm 148:2 we find that a parallel term to "hosts" is angels. Angels themselves are regarded as components of the *exousia,* part of the powers or the hosts. In Psalm 81:1 the pagan gods are even considered to be part of the hosts of the Lord. The Lord rules over the pagan gods and in Job 1:6-12 even Satan himself is regarded as part of the hosts, the *exousia* over which God rules.

Recalling our earlier discussion about Jesus' lordship over the principalities and powers, we can now observe that the New Testament teaches that Jesus has become Lord over all these *exousiai,* over all these forces or powers which operate in the world. All of these powers in the heavenly court were designed to function as servants of God's purpose, whether they be winds, temporal governments, angels, or Satan himself. But these powers can also become autonomous and rebellious, thus resisting God's purposes and work against Him. This precisely was the story of Satan. This precisely was the story of Germany under the Third Reich. Thus, although these powers are ultimately and finally ordained of God, they may at any given time in history refuse, deny, and rebel against God's rule which is now manifest in the lordship of Jesus Christ. Acts 2:36.

The New Testament affirms that regardless of the response of these powers, Jesus is Lord. Ultimately because of Jesus' resurrection and exaltation, all of these powers will be overcome. Because the Christian derives his ethics from the kingdom reality and lordship of Christ, he therefore lives in accord with that reality now. He looks at temporal government and even at Satan with the awareness, the hope, and the assurance that they are overcome. They have been defeated! Jesus alone is Lord and consequently it is this that motivates his peace witness in and through the ongoing political entities which now exist. He never accepts them as final or ultimate in authority. He knows their temporal character and readily condemns them for any ultimate aspirations.

It is in this setting that Romans 13 is to be understood. At no place does the Bible say that these powers are either good or bad in and of themselves. What the Bible does say is that they have been stripped of any ultimate power. Colossians 2:15. The Bible gives us neither a theory of politics nor a blanket sanction of any one political order. It proclaims rather the fact of an ultimate power, Jesus Christ, who calls for ultimate commitment and provides for the Christian an independent, transtemporal stance from which to witness to the quest for peace in time awaiting eternity.

The Romans 13 passage does say that "the authorities are ministers of God" (verse 6). But this statement is immediately qualified by the phrase which is best translated from the Greek as "when they attend to this very thing." This qualification draws into focus certain criteria against which the performance of the authorities is to be measured and judged. These criteria are mentioned in the first part of both verses 3 and 4: "For rulers are not a terror to good conduct, but to bad . . . for he is God's servant for your good." Precisely at this point does the Christian peacemaker find a responsibility; namely, to help define in contemporary, specific, political possibilities the situational meaning of good and bad. He does this not because he has great faith in political machinery but because those attached to Jesus Christ should know better than anyone else what the terms "good" and "bad" mean in the halls of human life and action.

Whereas in Romans 13 the government is viewed as potentially achieving a commendable function in the political realm, the Book of Revelation portrays the political powers in major rebellion and defiance of God's intended purpose for them. Some commentators suggest that in 2 Thessalonians 2 the temporal power is regarded as at one time the "restrainer of lawlessness" and at another time the very demonic "lawless one." With or without this interpretation, the point emerges that governments are not to be described in static moral terms. They are merely better or worse, more or less faithful to the divine purpose. Ideally the government is to command the obedience, respect, and tax support of all its subjects and citizens. 1 Peter 2:13-17. Whether or not this ideal and intention is realized by government is another question. If it is not realized, the Christian though subject to the authorities (taking whatever consequences follow) may need to disobey the government. Indeed he does have the mandate and the responsibility to give wherever possible a witness to the government in accord with the lordship of Christ so that government might be improved and more closely aligned with the purposes of God for it.

Morality

Another of the problems in discussing the church's peace-salting responsibility in the social order is understanding God's moral expectation of man. The question might be focused thus: Does God have two ultimate moral codes—one for the church and one for the government?

So far as the Scripture teaching is concerned we know of no such dichotomous plan on the part of God. Rather, all morality is rooted in the ethical norms of the gospel of Jesus Christ. In Romans 2:14-16 the Apostle Paul indicates that the pagan who never heard of the law or the gospel may by chance do what the law requires and thus be in a better position for final judgment than the pagan who lives a more wicked life or the Jew or Christian who knowing the moral norm of the gospel fails to live in accord with it. But the final point of this passage is that ultimately all will be judged by the one gospel norm, the ethical norm revealed in the life of Jesus Christ. This, of course, means then that men falling short of obedience to the ethical norm of the gospel have no autonomous ethical norm which God ultimately sanctions.

This, of course, has implications for the expected morality which characterizes government policy. Christians cannot expect government to exemplify moral norms which have been given for the church's obedience. At the same time, however, Christians may expect a better-than-now-is performance from government. There is always the possibility of men outside the gospel to do better than they are doing. Consequently the church when it addresses the government speaks in terms of specific alternatives. It speaks about specific possibilities for the government which are not being followed but which could be followed and which would more closely approximate the norms which we know they will never attain.

The chief reason why Christians must speak in relationship to specific alternatives is because the Bible does not teach any political theory which Christians should try to sell to government. While Christians may advise certain political actions which they believe to more closely approximate the Christian ethic, yet they can never propose a form or theory of government in the name of Christ. All that the Christian has to propose is the kingdom of God. And that proposal is for a radically new order in society which involves allocation of the government order to secondary significance.

The church's mission then with regard to the morality of government is to pray and witness in order that the highest morality possible might be achieved. With Paul we believe that some levels of morality, or immorality, are preferable to others and are more amenable to the judgment of God. This accords with our findings in the previous point that it is meaningful and important to observe that governments may carry on their work more or less in accord with the purpose and plan of God. This purpose and plan is never the kingdom of God realized through government structure but it is the quest for the more amenable political policies possible so that the Christian gospel can be advanced and God's mercy and justice more closely approximated in the temporal order.

War

To sharpen the issue, we pose the question: Is war wrong or is war wrong only for the church and not for the government? This, of course, is implicitly answered by the foregoing discussion on the biblical view of morality. For outside the moral norm of the gospel, all other action, though we may call it more or less moral, is actually more or less immoral. And within this realm of immorality there has been war, is war, and will continue to be war. This does not make war right. It only underscores the fact that war is and sin is. The reason why war continues is because of human sin, man's rebellion against the lordship of Christ. War continues because God's norm of morality as revealed in the gospel of Jesus Christ is ignored, denied, and refused. From a theological viewpoint then, based upon the New Testament teaching, all war is sin and wrong.

In the history of the Christian church there have been ways, however, in which war has been supposedly justified. Chief among these is the just war theory. This theory seeks to make war in certain cases a legitimate activity of God's people. In today's world this theory is no longer widely held. Many theologians and ethicists question whether there ever was a just war, whether this theory ever was tenable, and whether any war was fought for a holy cause. From the theological viewpoint there is a wide consensus that war has always been wrong, continues to be wrong, and always will be wrong.

However, from a political viewpoint, the major opinion of theologians and ethicists yields a different emphasis. Many theologians and ethicists contend that war is politically necessary as a way of balancing man's evil egoisms. This viewpoint, known as Christian realism, has been well argued and advanced by Reinhold Niebuhr and many of his supporting ethicists. This viewpoint contends that war is a fact of political necessity, but though necessary, it is never right. These ethicists will even say that when we engage in war, we do compromise the gospel norm. But we can do no other. We trust for God's forgiveness.

From this perspective of analysis some wars, however, may be unnecessary and *therefore* wrong, not only in a theological sense but also in a political sense. This is the situation of the present moment. Many ethicists and Christians outside the realm of Anabaptist-Mennonite ethics feel that on the basis of political, not theological, judgment, the war in Vietnam is unnecessary. Therefore it is immoral even in the realm of political ethics which are ethics of necessity for the temporal order. This is why we often hear statements such as: "The war in Vietnam is immoral and unjust." That statement can be made as a consequence of the theological assertion above—that all wars are wrong and sinful and therefore this one war is immoral and unjust. But it can also be made as a consequence of a political judgment. Such a statement then does not derive from the previous premise that all wars are wrong and sinful but from the premise that some wars are necessary; others are unnecessary; and this war is of the latter kind. Therefore it is immoral and wrong.

What then does this discussion mean for our presence in the political order as nonresistant Christians? It means that all war is wrong and sinful. This witness and affirmation should be continuously proclaimed in the realm of government. It is an indiscriminate call to repentance and full obedience to the way of Christ and to a primary allegiance to the kingdom community.

It also means that we should in fidelity to our peace-salting mission discover how to witness against a war that is popularly judged politically unnecessary and therefore morally wrong even in the political context. The crucial question confronting the church today is how to speak on this second level without distorting the quality of our trans-situational witness?

Methods of Peacemaking

God called Israel to be a "kingdom of priests" (Exodus 19:5) and a "light to the nations" (Isaiah 49:6). When we look at Israel's ethics we therefore derive some notion of the direction in which God was leading them as they were fulfilling their salting responsibility among the nations.

In Exodus 21:21-24 we read about the "eye for eye" and "tooth for tooth" law of retaliation. Superficially it appears as though Israel is being told by God to make sure that you get a square amount of vengeance. Actually, however, in their societal context this command was a limitation to vengeance. It restricted the amount of vengeance that could be meted out against the aggressor. The human impulse would be to retaliate by two eyes for one eye but the divine command was a limitation of retaliation.

Later in the Old Testament period the prophets called for an ethic of social justice which paved the way for the radical love ethic of the New Testament. The passages which should be studied are Isaiah 58; Micah 6:1-8; Amos 5:21-26. In these passages the prophetic ethic challenges Israel to seek after a way of justice, mercy, and love in all of their community relationships. Prophets Isaiah and Micah even envision an end of war and the reign of peace fully manifested upon the earth. Isaiah 30:15; 31:1-3; 2:1-4; Micah 4:1-7.

Another significant Old Testament stream of thought is the prophets oracles against the foreign nations. For the most part these oracles were in forms of judgment against the foreign nations. Whether they were ever sent or delivered to the nation's headquarters is a matter of speculation. But one thing is certain: the prophets were concerned about the moral responsibility of all the nations. A good many chapters in Isaiah, Jeremiah, and Ezekiel were composed of oracles addressed to the foreign nations. This certainly indicates that no power stands outside accountability to God's ethical will for men.

From the New Testament we have already observed God's ultimate will for man. Now we must observe how the early church carried out their responsibility of being the salt and the leaven of the society in which they lived. The Book of Acts abounds with examples of how the church practiced a norm of life which undoubtedly influenced the surrounding society. In the early chapters of the book the Christians developed a brotherhood which took seriously economic sharing among the brotherhood. Interchanging this theme of economic sharing is the theme of direct encounter with the political authorities. In Acts 4, 5 and climactically in chapter 7, the church chose fidelity to the gospel of Jesus Christ at the cost of civil disobedience and civil punishment. Chapter 5 affirms, "We must obey God rather than men" (verse 29). Chapter 7 describes the first martyrdom of the Christian church resulting from political conflict and disobedience. It is not insignificant that both Jesus and Paul were ultimately condemned and killed on charges of incipient political treason, creating riots, stirring up the people, refusing to support the status quo expectations of society.

The gospel is indeed revolutionary. It never is content to endorse the status quo structures of society. It calls its followers to a radical faithfulness which ever challenges the sub-ethical standards of society. Indeed the New Testament records critical attitudes toward social, economic, and political policy. In Luke 13:32 Jesus calls Herod a fox. In Mark 6:18 John the Baptist condemns Herod for marrying his brother's wife. In Acts 22:25 Paul questions the legality of the Roman tribunal's judgment. In Acts 24:25 Paul argues with Felix about "justice and self-control and future judgment." The early church took seriously its mission to transcend and defy existing structures of social, economic, and political order. Not because of pragmatic reasons, not because it had some superior political theory, but precisely because it understood the gospel of Jesus Christ.

In conclusion, the objective of the peace witness is to "overcome evil with good" (Romans 12:21) through loving all men, even the "enemy," and praying "for those who persecute" us. Matthew 5:43-48. Such a peace witness springs from our commitment to the gospel of our Lord Jesus Christ. The gospel itself becomes the criterion by which we decide what we should say and how we should say it. Concern to be faithful witnesses to the gospel takes priority over questions of pragmatic policy and effective results. The validity of the method through which we choose to speak depends upon the Christian integrity and the authenticity of the person and group who speak.

While we reflect upon the various methods which we might employ in witnessing to the political orders, let us not forget the ultimate question: By what method does God speak His will to temporal government? Paul in Ephesians 3:10 would answer: "through the church."

VOICES OF HOPE

Toward a New Understanding
of Nonresistance

When I became a member of the local branch of the National Association for the Advancement of Colored People in Kansas City, Kansas, I found them discussing at their regular monthly meetings the problems the Negro has with employment, housing, hospital care, education, and contacts with local churches. Like NAACP groups across the country in the 1960's this group was becoming more militant, using direct action, and no longer limiting itself to taking grievances to court in expensive lawsuits and successive appeals to higher courts. The only other white member who attended meetings when I joined was a Catholic clergyman. Catholics who were a few years beyond the middle age could remember from their childhood the burning crosses of Klansmen at their homes and churches in Kansas City, Kansas. In the 1960's they were the first church group to become involved in righting wrongs done to Negroes in that city.

My education about the church's role in race relations and the usefulness of a doctrine like nonresistance began immediately. At an NAACP meeting we were discussing school desegregation. Among other practices the school board was hiring buses to carry Negro children from the Negro ghetto in our parish, driving past two white grade schools, to a small understaffed and underequipped Negro grade school. My contribution at this meeting was to make the remark that we should inform the churches of the city about the issue and get their help to work for a change. Everybody had

This chapter reprinted by permission from *Mennonite Life*, January 1967.

a good laugh and the meeting resumed. I was not quite convinced then, but months later I realized I had said something pretty funny. Churches that taught love and even nonresistance were not being persecuted and felt no need to re-evaluate the doctrine that one should love one's enemies or that one should be using nonresistance in dealings with a foe. They felt they had no enemies. It was almost as if the churches had planned their indifference to drive the Negro to the violence that erupted later. Presumably after the Negro attacked them, then the doctrines of loving the enemy and nonresistance could be applied and they would then forgive the Negro his wrongs to them.

By 1961 I felt that nonresistance as I had always understood it (turning the other cheek, avoiding fights) had proved its value. The church's Sunday school, boys' club, vacation Bible school, weekday church school were integrated and we had begun to integrate our membership. Negroes in our neighborhood had their own preferences and convictions and they were not desperately trying to join a white church. There were, however, a few looking for a church home in their own neighborhood who were willing to venture into the painful embarrassing slips, the glad relief as old myths are shattered, and the side by side efforts that go with integrated membership. Our church office received a few calls from other suburban congregations asking for help to set up interracial dialogues. I received two awards for interracial work and was even asked to represent the Negro viewpoint, even though I was not a Negro, in some of the discussions that took place at city hall concerning racial controversy and the poverty program. My role was that of a go-between helping the two sides that seemed to misunderstand each other, to speak to each other.

If this was nonresistance, this friendly handshaking on both sides of the conflict, the Mennonite forefathers who found that it led to suffering must have had some kind of personality problems because I was finding it a popular way to live, having friendships on both sides of the controversy, some honors, and only an occasional protest from neighbors who felt that associating with Negroes was wrong.

At the same time, the experience of having our boys' club turned away from the YMCA pool several times, having the same club dropped from a baseball league before the season began because we had Negro players, seeing friends and parishioners humiliated at the restaurant next door to our church, and seeing how a city pushes Negro youth out of the school and out of the neighborhoods the whites want, provided plenty of grounds for a guilty conscience for a go-between. Mennonites can see that the doctrine of nonresistance phrased to bring reconciliation in boundary line arguments between two landowners and to prevent fruitless court squabbles has to be restated in the new situations where God had led us.

"Staying Out of Fights"?

The change most obvious in the understanding of nonresistance is that one cannot be satisfied with the go-between role that I had drifted into. One has to choose sides. One cannot, for example, take the role the pope is described as having taken in World War II in the play, "The Deputy." In this role the pope accepted both the Nazis and the persecuted Jews and supported them both. The pope sympathized and understood both sides but did not openly declare himself opposed to the Nazis or a defender of the Jews. It is the same role taken by moderates in the South and many of us in the North. However, if a person has not chosen sides and identified himself with the oppressed, the doctrine of nonresistance (turning the other cheek) is wrong for him. Nonresistance is a doctrine for one who is offended or attacked, not for the "umpire" or the "go-between."

If a person does not "choose sides" and stand with those he feels God has shown him to be the oppressed, he can say, "Love your enemies," but both sides know he does not have to care about them to say that. If a person on one side or the other says to his fellow battlers, "Turn the other cheek" or "Love your enemies," this statement means something.

The person who has chosen sides can also be forgiving to those on the other side because he has taken sides, has been offended, and has something to forgive. If he is only an "umpire," he has nothing to forgive. To put it more strongly, he cannot be a reconciler unless he has taken sides. He can only be an umpire.

The biblical description of this is God's action in which He tries to reconcile man to Himself by sending His leaders and prophets to them. Finally, as the New Testament relates, He comes Himself, takes a position, is offended, and forgives men. An all-powerful God had little to forgive until He Himself was involved, offended, and threatened when He was powerless. Likewise, Jesus in Luke 4:14 f. chooses the side He sees to be the oppressed.

Reconciling Requirements

When one chooses sides, he has the possibility of being a reconciler. Until he does, a Christian is in danger of taking over the state's role as a court or a federal mediator, hearing both sides and forcing some kind of agreement or settlement. This umpire is needed and the state does it as best it can. The Christian's role, however, is one of reconciliation. We see God at work reconciling men to Himself and men to each other. Our mission is to work with God at this same work, not by umpiring, but by reconciling our differences, not someone else's differences, with others.

I am not saying that the Christian must choose sides in a labor-management conflict, the marital conflict of a husband and wife, or the cold war between China and the United States. It is not easy for us to see in such cases who is the oppressed and who is the oppressor or whose propaganda we should believe. It is often the case that both are at fault. However, when God shows us as clearly as He has in America that it is wrong to continue the oppression of Negroes, Christians are no longer allowed to take the umpire role saying, "You should not be fighting," or "Please, please let's not do this here." Neither is he allowed to merely be an understander.

It should also be noted that when one chooses the side of the oppressed, this does not mean he is choosing the side of the people who always do right and just acts and do not ever take revenge. Standing with the Negro does not free the Negro from human feelings, hatefulness, or from doing illegal acts of vengeance. One who stands with the Negro and finds himself involved in things he does not condone, will have to share the blame when his side does wrong, ask for God's forgiveness, and keep on working at the reconciling task. There are, of course, things he cannot participate in and activities which his group does that he must speak out against. The point is that a Christian cannot refuse to choose sides because he feels that both sides do wrong and neither side is good enough for him.

A Reformulation of Nonresistance

If nonresistance was no longer to be interpreted as "don't cause anybody any trouble" and now meant that one chose the side of the oppressed, in order to be a reconciler what would the result be? A test came in July 1965. Like those in the seminary community at Elkhart, Indiana, a member in the Fort Wayne Mennonite congregation and in the Topeka Mennonite congregation, and many others, my wife and I decided to sell our home in a white community through a Negro realtor. (In Kansas City a Negro realtor is called a realatist.) The buyer was Henry Goodson, a Negro raising his family in a house the city would have condemned if it would have been vacant and they would not have been in a position of forcing a man out of his house and being unable to find a place for him to go. The street on which he lived was unpaved as were many of the streets in his area, and in fact cars could no longer use a part of it. The ghetto in which he lived used septic tanks for their sewage, although all the surrounding areas of the city were able to use the city sewage system. The plea that children should go to a neighborhood school did not apply to this community and they were bussed out of the neighborhood to a Negro school in another Negro ghetto two and a half miles away.

I let my neighbors know that I was using a Negro realtor so that the house would be open to anyone as, of course, it should be in America. When Henry Goodson bought it after several people, white and Negro, had looked at it, I visited my neighbors with a written letter to sit down and explain our action. I had not asked my neighbors whether they would mind having a Negro neighbor before I sold the house because I did not feel that this was a moral thing to do and because I felt that I might anger them too much by going against the advice white neighborhoods like ours feel they should give.

In this case the "sides" between which we could choose were on the one hand our Negro friends and church members who felt housing should be open to all. On the other were our white friends and a few church members and many people that I never knew who felt selling a house in a white community to a Negro was all right but a Christian should not do it because it hurts his neighbors. In a choice between offending the next door neighbors and keeping Henry Goodson's family in the neighborhood that was deprived of good schools, scout troops, YMCA clubs, and which had its share of polluted streams that ran down the streets from overrunning cesspools, some felt that it would be better not to offend my next door neighbors. On the other hand, I felt that most people would choose as I did if they would have been fortunate enough to have been in on the NAACP meetings that discussed these problems and would have been patiently taught the realities of urban life.

My job, if I was no longer an umpire, was to absorb the hate (the phone calls at night, the threats to my children, the hint from the city official that I had better not ask the police for assistance if I got in trouble, "the visit" from a group of young men one night who after a little shouting left a white peaked hood on my door, and the other kinds of harassment familiar in our present racial conflict). I could teach in the Freedom School to Negro youngsters "love your enemies" because I had shared some of the hatred which they are subjected to. I could go through the painful process of reconciliation to white neighbors and white real-estate developers who started the harassing campaign because I had been offended and had something to forgive. In other words, I could be the reconciler instead of the umpire.

Six months ago, almost a year after Henry Goodson had moved into my home, we revisited our old neighborhood. We made the visit, not because we were anxious to go through those painful reconciling attempts again, but because we knew that this was something we should do. By this time, the Goodsons were well liked by their next door neighbors and many on the street were a little proud they had weathered the storm and had learned some new things about what a neighbor is. Reconciliation was a reality.

Conclusions

1. The new meaning of nonresistance that I am learning at this stage of my pilgrimage is that it is based on the incarnation, the fact that Christ dwelt among us and identified with people. Nonresistance to be practiced means that Mennonites must first agree to come into the world and live in it as Christ did. If this first requirement of nonresistance cannot be met, this doctrine that we prize so highly will be the cause of our downfall. Nonresistance will then become a cruel practice of being friendly to both the oppressor and the oppressed, but refusing the painful role of reconciler.

2. Nonresistance as a doctrine means a way to do the reconciling work that God does and calls us to do. Nonresistance does not mean being an umpire but it means being a reconciler. Reconciliation is possible only if one has chosen sides and stood with the oppressed.

3. This interpretation of nonresistance means that Mennonites must learn about nonresistance from a group outside themselves. We do not have in our recent history the kind of experience that we need. Our history tells us to stay out of fights, a right way of reconciliation in many situations in the past. The new situation means that we will have to go through the painful role of learning that we have only a partial gospel to contribute, and will have to

learn from non-Mennonites what the rest of it is so that both Mennonites and non-Mennonites can find salvation. It would seem obvious that Mennonite missionaries and voluntary service workers in the South, in South America, in Asia, or wherever they might be, need to choose the side of the oppressed if they are going to proclaim the reconciling word of God. It is not known how long the oppressed, the American Negro, for example, is willing to be the patient teacher.

It seems very important, if we are not to proclaim a false gospel about reconciliation, that all proclaimers of this word in this country and abroad identify with the oppressed and let us know when they return to our churches to give reports, when we as oppressors do the oppression. The church in England did not identify with the laboring man when he was going through his struggles to gain a decent and wholesome life for himself and his children and the churches of England are now empty. If we lost such opportunities, it is hard to know how many more opportunities God will be willing to give us.

10/   BY JOHN HOWARD YODER

The Way of the Peacemaker *

Peacemaking in a democratic society involves two fundamental issues. First there is the broad ethical question: How should Christians properly behave? By "Christians" I mean here what we try to take the word to mean in careful theology; not simply church-goers, or participants in the organized life of American denominational Christianity. Nor do I mean simply people who happen to live in a country that calls itself Christian, in the sense that everybody who lives in Sweden is a Lutheran—but rather persons whose sincere confession is that Jesus Christ is Lord. How should Christians—people defined this way—behave in a world in which violence, enmity, and international conflict are part of the situation? How should we serve this Jesus whom we call Lord, the man in whose cross God has reconciled the world to Himself, thus making of His disciples ministers of reconciliation? How should we follow the Jesus Christ of the resurrection, by whose spirit the disciples can live a new kind of life, who instructs His disciples to love friend and foe alike?

And then there is a second set of questions, to which our society right now is trying to find answers. As citizens of a democratic society, we live in a nation which has as we noted before many churchgoers, but where there are not many people (here I'm not speaking judgmentally, for any observer would say the same thing) who are letting their lives be dictated by their loyalty to Jesus Christ. At the same time we are citizens of a world society in

°This chapter is taken from a taped address given at the Embury Methodist Church in Freeport, Ill.

which even the people who are only nominally Christian are a minority, getting smaller proportionately. We can't assume that most people are living lives dictated by Jesus Christ; we can't assume that the people to whom we speak, or whom we are trying to help make a decision, are committed to forsaking all and following Jesus. The people we are talking to are rather, people exercising power and seeking power so that they can exercise more. How do we function as human beings in this kind of world, when social groups try to make decisions?

On this level of what we might call secular political decision, Vietnam is a special case. Every case is different in the details of how we can go about evaluating it. The war of national liberation in Vietnam is not the same in the mind of most Americans as the war of national liberation of 1776, where most of American society tells us the rebels were on the right side, or the war of national liberation of 1861, where our schoolbooks tell us that the rebels were on the wrong side, but for different reasons. Dean Rusk is not the same thing as Ho Chi Minh. Every factor in a secular political decision is different every time. What a government does differs according to whether it is working at home in the area of its own sovereignty, where it is trying to produce a just social order, an ordered state, or whether it is on the other side of the globe, trying to be a policeman to keep what it calls law and order in somebody else's backyard.

Now these two topics are interlaced. You can never really separate them, especially since Constantine, who "Christianized" the Roman Empire at the point of a sword, and since Charlemagne, who Christianized the rest of Europe at the point of a sword, and since the pilgrim fathers, who started Christianizing the United States at the point of a sword. With this heritage, there have always been religious people who wanted to support their government, including its wars. There have always been persons in government who wanted the support of the church for whatever they were doing, and there have always been church people willing to give that support. So there has been a tradition of getting along well together between church and state in the western society.

We've changed that progressively in the last 200 years on this continent. Yet with all the progress in religious liberty and separation of church and state, there remain many complicated interrelations with these two kinds of questions.

War and Common Sense

What are the considerations with regard to war and peace that anyone ought to be able to see, regardless of Christian faith? This first set of questions is not what matters for Christian ethics, but we have to be able to label them in order to be aware of where they are on the map.

There are considerations which we can call "common sense." They have to do with the way anyone's mind works. One way to test any question is to turn it around and ask, How would it look if you were on the other side? What would we have thought at the time of the famous U-2 incident if it had been a Russian spy plane that was shot down over northern Illinois? Would we have been as sure as President Eisenhower was at that time, that the other party shouldn't have made any fuss over this because, after all, they were obliged to spy?

In the case of Cuba, how did it happen that it was so traumatically frightening to discover that there were going to be communist missiles 100 miles from Miami, when for half a generation already, the same kind of American missiles had been at the Russian border in Turkey? It didn't occur to us that the Russians had any right to object until they turned the tables.

If we were now to use the example of the Vietnam war, how would it really look to us if there were 500,000 Chinese in the southern half of Mexico, placed there because there were 50,000 North Mexicans infiltrating into South Mexico and the Chinese wanted to keep the North Mexicans from North Mexico from upsetting the regime of other North Mexicans whom they were supporting as a puppet government in South Mexico, and if they were stopping the infiltration by bombing the border at El Paso? How would that feel? This kind of thinking is just common sense

—it isn't Christian thinking, it isn't unchristian thinking; it's just being human from the other side, putting yourself in the other position and trying to imagine how it looks. Turn about is fair play!

Another kind of common sense argument is usually identified with the old French phrase *noblesse oblige*. If you claim a certain honor, a certain nobility, then that obliges you to something. If a communist believes that might makes right and that terror is a good way to spread his form of government, it makes sense, because it fits his theory. But if we claim that government by the consent of the governed is necessary, and that human personality must be respected, then we can't use the same methods. If we commit ourselves to higher values, then we must be judged by those higher values, and we can't justify doing everything that the other party does.

There is the kind of common sense that asks whether it is ever proper for someone to be judge and jury in his own case, which is of course what you do when you decide whether it is your duty to police the other side of the world.

The Just War

The most careful line of thought about war and peace is traditionally known as the theory of the just war. This is an ancient way of thinking which many people of our peace churches want to throw out the window completely. It is essential to begin by respecting the honesty of those who seek to think carefully at this point. Likewise it is important to distinguish between some reasons for war that you can make a just case for and others you cannot make a case for. If you are not in one of the historic peace churches, then the chances are that the official position of your denomination is that although some wars may be justifiable, others are not, and that Christians should distinguish between the two so they can be ready to serve in the one, but not in the other. It is thus the duty of the Christian according to Presbyterian, Episcopalian, Lutheran ideas to look at a given military operation and ask, "Is that justifiable?" and if it is not, not to participate.

There are three criteria that are traditionally used in this way of thinking. One is "just authority." A just war cannot be waged by a bandit, nor by a private citizen. It must be waged by a legitimate government. Let us use the Vietnam example, not to pass a final judgment on the Vietnam case, but to illustrate the logic. We would ask in North America, where the constitution says that any declaration of war must be made by the congress, whether it is proper for half a million soldiers to be committed to a military operation in a foreign country without meeting that constitutional requirement. We have to ask whether the Tonkin Bay Resolution makes up for that. Next we would have to ask whether the Saigon government, the Ky regime, was a just authority when it came into power as one of a long series of armed overthrows of the previous governments, each of which had also been set up by an overthrow of the previous government. Next we should ask whether that really is changed very much now that there has been an election in which only those people could vote who didn't challenge the Ky regime and in which the Ky regime even then got only 35 percent of the vote. Is the Ky-Thieu regime a government of the people which has the right then to fight a justifiable war?

The next kind of question asks for the "just cause." It is justifiable to fight a war to reestablish peace, to defend law and order. It is not justifiable, according to the ancient Christian thinking on this subject, to fight a war for a holy cause; a religious war or a crusade. The Lutheran Augsburg Confession, the Presbyterian Westminster Confession, and the Episcopalian Thirty-nine Articles, and the other standard confessions of the Protestant tradition, allow for a justifiable war but reject the crusade. Well, are we fighting in Vietnam to restore peace and order in South Vietnam, or to stop communism around the world? The former would make a justifiable case; the latter would not, according to just war theory.

Third, a "just war" must be fought according to "just means." The criterion of just means will distinguish between civilian and military objectives. At what point does a war cease to be justified because it makes more refugees than the people it saves? Instead of counting that a military operation is successful because it gained a certain amount of territory which it will be possible to hold, the measurement which is now used in Vietnam is a body count—we don't say person count, or soul count, just body count, depersonalizing the other party and making a virtue of what earlier thinking about war considered a vice, the maximum amount of lethal effect.

Now these are not denominational arguments. This consideration has no link to Brethren, or Friends, or Mennonite thought. This is the denominational position of Presbyterians, Congregationalists, Episcopalians, Methodists, and Lutherans. These people are committed by their creedal statements to applying this kind of criterion honestly. My first question is then whether those who are not pacifists will in our day have the concern and the honesty, whether they are Christian or not, but especially if they are, whether they be veterans of foreign wars or hippies, not for the sake of denominational loyalty, but just out of ordinary human decency and logic, to use this kind of test. Now we move to the central issue, the context of specific Christian loyalty.

Jesus and War

Here we would begin with a study of Jesus and war. I've chosen to look simply at a few selected passages from the New Testament as portrayals of the attitude which fits with the gospel. They are all passages which illuminate the quality of the Christian life in a world of conflict, in a way that has implications including the question of war.

First observe these words from Luke 6, part of the Sermon on the Plain,

> Love your enemies, do good to those who hate you, bless those who curse you, pray for those who abuse you. To him who strikes you on the cheek, offer the other also; and from him who takes away your cloak do not withhold your coat as well. Give to every one who begs from you; and of him who

116

takes away your goods do not ask them again. And as you wish that men would do to you, do so to them. (Luke 6:27b-31, RSV)

Here, as is not the case in the similar Matthew story, reasons are provided:

If you love those who love you, what credit is that to you? For even sinners love those who love them. And if you do good to those who do good to you, what credit is that to you? For even sinners do the same. And if you lend to those from whom you hope to receive, what credit is that to you? Even sinners lend to sinners, to receive as much again. But love your enemies, and do good, and lend, expecting nothing in return; and your reward will be great, and you will be sons of the Most High; for he is kind to the ungrateful and the selfish. Be merciful, even as your Father is merciful. (Luke 6:32-36, RSV)

The striking thing about this explanation that Jesus gives for loving your enemies is the repeated argument, "What thank have ye?" (in the King James language) or "What credit is that to you?" It is interesting that Jesus asks the question that way. He takes for granted, He assumes, that there should be something special about your behavior. It isn't enough to be just ordinarily good, to pay your bills and keep your promises and not hurt anybody. What is expected of the disciple is something extra. If you are good only the way everybody else is good, what credit is that? Now certainly, in the total context of the teaching of the gospel, when Jesus talks about "credit," He doesn't mean that we are earning our way into God's favor—He doesn't mean that it's by loving our neighbors, or loving our enemies, that we are going to merit some kind of reward. He means, "If you love only those who love you, what is there about your behavior that communicates the gospel?" What is there about what you are doing that reflects anything about God? What is there about your attitude to others that portrays the

117

character of the love of God, if your love goes only as far as the other guy?

The second thing that Jesus says by way of interpretation and explanation is, "you will be sons of the Most High; for he is kind to the ungrateful and the selfish." In other words, your character will portray the character of God. And what is God's character? Precisely that His love extends to those who don't merit it, and who don't give thanks for it, that God's goodness toward men is not conditioned, is not limited, is not merited, is not calculated on the basis of how much love men have coming. Your love is to be the same way if you are to be His children. ┘

So Jesus is talking about a kind of life, a kind of ethic which will be a reflection in human affairs of that character of God which we call "grace," namely, that His goodness is not limited by what we have coming. The application of this is that your enemy should have just as much of your love as your friend. It isn't because there is a rule in the Book somewhere that says something like that. It isn't because there's a rule in the Old Testament that says, "Thou shalt not kill." It's because of the quality of God's own character. Matthew's Gospel says this in the Sermon on the Mount at the end of chapter 5 in even stronger words: "be perfect, as your heavenly Father is perfect." Now here we can get off the track by discussing the doctrine of perfection. Some argue that the whole point of the Sermon on the Mount is not to prove that we should be perfect, but to prove to us that we shouldn't be, because we know we can't be, and the point of the demand is just to make us recognize our guilt. But this isn't the subject at all. "Perfection" in this context means something much more simple than that, and much more possible. God does not discriminate between those who merit His love and those who don't. You too shall be undiscriminating, unlimiting in your love.

> Now great multitudes accompanied him; and he turned and said to them, "If any one comes to me and does not hate his own father and mother and wife and children and brothers

and sisters, yes, and even his own life, he cannot be my disciple. Whoever does not bear his own cross and come after me, cannot be my disciple. For which of you, desiring to build a tower—"

Following this is the story of the one man who wanted to build a tower and hadn't counted the cost, and the other man who wanted to win a war and hadn't counted the cost.

> So therefore, whoever of you does not renounce all that he has cannot be my disciple. (14:25-33, RSV)

We know the passage about bearing the cross because we have it in the other Gospels as well. We know the warning about not beginning something without being able to finish it. This is not new. Nor is our point now to define what you have to give up, or what it means to hate your father and mother. The deep and new truth is what it says about the context of all Christian ethics. Following Jesus is not for everybody. It is for those who have consciously chosen to give up something in order to follow Jesus. Now what does that have to do with the war problem? Something very profound and far-reaching. One of the most common assumptions of moral thought in our society in the last 200 years has been that whatever you say is right or wrong for yourself, you must be willing to generalize. So if I say as a Christian that I must love my enemies, that I cannot kill, the very first question that comes back is, "Well, what if everybody did that?" Can everybody do that? Can you ask that of everybody? And if everybody did it, would it work? Could you save the country? This is the normal reflex of people in our society. We check a decision by whether everybody can do it, or whether you can ask it of everybody. The great German philosopher Immanuel Kant, who lived two centuries ago, called this way of thinking the categorical imperative. You test any statement by whether you can ask it of everybody. If you cannot ask it of everybody, it must not be right.

This certainly has a lot to do with the war discussion, at least the way we have usually encountered it. The first question is, "How could you save America if everybody did that?" or "Can you ask everybody to do that? Will they have the devotion, or the conviction, or will they have the vision to pay the price?" Jesus cuts off at the root this whole kind of reasoning by saying that Christian discipleship is for only a few people who have counted the cost and have left behind many valuable things. He doesn't say there is anything wrong or evil with father or mother, or brother or sister, or houses and lands. No, those are very wonderful things to have; but still you're just going to have to leave them behind if you want to follow Him. And so it is that in Christian ethics, proper Christian ethics, speaking with great theological clarity, we must simply stop asking, "Will it work for everyone?" There is no chance that everybody will try it. That's a meaningless question. The real question is: "Will it be redemptive if it is done by a few?" There will only ever be a few anyway. I don't say this out of philosophical pessimism; I say it out of statistical realism.

The other need we remind ourselves of in this passage is to be clear how every disciple is to bear his own cross. Now the cross of Jesus was not any old kind of suffering. It was not, for instance, a kind of suffering that He earned, a just penalty. Nor was it suffering like sickness, where you never quite know what hit you. There are two kinds of experiences we most often call "cross" in modern pastoral counseling. One is a difficult social situation, a grumpy mother-in-law or an unruly child or something else in the family that is hard to live with and you can't get away from; the other is sickness. Jesus' cross was not mother-in-law trouble or sickness. The cross of Christ was a clear, expectable, predictable, normal result of a fact that in a world that didn't want His kind of man around, He was God's kind of man, teaching God's truth and living God's kind of life right in the middle of a society that could not stand for that. That's why He was put to death. The cross of the Christian must, if we are to have the right to use the word, have about it something of the same character. It must be suffering that comes upon the disciple of Jesus because of his obedience, because of his sharing consciously, knowing what he was doing, in the character of Christ's work in the world.

Our final passage from Luke is right in the middle of the Lord's Supper story. Although we have similar texts in Matthew and Mark, it occurs somewhat earlier in these accounts.

In the Matthew story, the question is raised by Mrs. Zebedee, who wants to make sure her boys will get cabinet positions. In Luke's account this same question was being debated in the mid-. dle of the Last Supper experience itself. Even in this communion experience the disciples were grumbling about which of them would be regarded as the greatest.

> And he said to them, "The kings of the Gentiles exercise lordship over them; and those in authority over them are called benefactors. But not so with you; rather let the greatest among you become as the youngest, and the leader as one who serves. For which is the greater, one who sits at table, or one who serves? Is it not the one who sits at table? But I am among you as one who serves." (Luke 22:25-27)

Jesus does not say it's a bad thing that in this world there are those who lord it over others. He just says it is that way. Among the Gentiles that's just the way it is. There is power. There is the wielding of power, and the people who wield power always tell you that it's for your good. They let themselves be called benefactors. It is always the case that the tyrant lets it be said that his wielding of power is as a benefactor.

Jesus does not say the world should be run otherwise. He does not say that if He were king He would do differently. He just says, This isn't the way it is going to be among My disciples. Not because of the Sermon on the Mount, or the Ten Commandments telling them not to kill, but because of the character of Jesus. I am a servant, and that is why you should be a servant, too. Or, as it is in Matthew's story, "Because I give my life a ransom, therefore you are not to be lords, but servants."

Now we have to ask, How does this link to present social discussions? Ever since Constantine, ever since the identification of Christianity with the success of a given country and culture and national government, it has been assumed that it is our business to make things come out right. This is like the position that I referred to earlier in the name of the philosopher Kant. His assumption is built into our society, into our emotional reflexes, our logical reflexes, the way we think when we aren't even conscious that we are using logic. So it is too with this Constantinian assumption that it's our business to make history come out right. If it doesn't come out right, we've shirked our responsibility. So we make our decisions by looking ahead and by calculating: "If I do A, B will follow, and if I do C, D will follow. Of course D would be worse than B; so I will do A."

We are so used to this mode of reasoning that it doesn't even occur to us that there might be some other way to think about making decisions. This is a model of decision in terms of sovereignty. It assumes I'm on top, so that if I go this way, history will go this way, and if I go that way, the course of human events will go that way. So I'm choosing the way human events are to go. This is the way Dean Rusk wakes up every morning. "Where shall I make events go?" Unfortunately it is also the way Ho Chi Minh wakes up every morning. So it never works. More than one person always makes decisions. Yet each decides as though he were the center of the universe. But that's still the logic we choose. If we turn the vanes this way, if we open these valves or open this channel, the course of history will go down this stream and that will be good. And if we do it the other way, the course of history will go down that stream, and that will be bad; so we do it this way. Moral decision is based first on the assumption that we can calculate the consequences, and second on the axiom that it's our business to make history come out right. But Jesus says, "No, it isn't your business to make things come out right; it isn't your business to bomb a nation; it isn't your business to be sovereign. I'm here to be a servant and you're to be here like Me, as a servant." Somebody else makes history come out right.

Now there are two responses to this New Testament picture of Jesus. We haven't really been talking about ethics all by itself, about right and wrong behavior, for their own sake; I've been talking about what Jesus said about the character of His life, which His disciples as well are going to bear.

One of these defensive responses is to say, Yes, that's all true of Jesus, but that's religious. Jesus had to die for our salvation, so that His cross was a particular religious event. The fact that He was nonviolent, for instance, or the fact that He refused to be king and was a servant instead, that He washed other people's feet, and even the fact that He healed and fed people does not mean that we should be servants and heal and feed others. Because, after all, Jesus was unique, wasn't He? Jesus was a revelation. Jesus came to die for men's salvation.

There are two considerations that keep us from admitting that the deity of Jesus keeps Him from being our example. One is that all of the New Testament writers tell us that we are to follow Him in His way.

The idea of imitating Jesus is not a very current idea in the New Testament, although we think it is because we are used to preaching it; and it isn't. Jesus was a carpenter, a craftsman, but nothing in the Bible says that we should be craftsmen. It never occurred to the apostles to prefer one particular kind of livelihood to another. Jesus was not married, but it never occurred to the apostles to say that we should follow Him in that. Even when in 1 Corinthians 7 Paul was arguing for not getting married, it didn't occur to him to appeal to the example of Jesus. Jesus didn't have a place to live; He lived off the charity of other people and walked around with a group of disciples who had a common purse—none of this is made normative in the New Testament. The only one thing about Jesus that is to be imitated according to the testimony of the apostles is what He did about evil, how He bore the cross, how He gave Himself for His enemies. And this every New Testament writer, with the possible exception of Jude, tells us we are to imitate.

The early church soon identified a heresy called the docetic heresy, the label given to those people who thought that Jesus was only a religious figure and not also a human being. It is a constant temptation for the church to think that the cross is a salvation event, but it isn't for us. The cross of Jesus, He tells us Himself and the apostles all confirm this later, is for us to follow. That's God's way of dealing with His enemies to give His life for them.

One temptation is to keep Jesus different by making the cross a spiritual event, which has nothing to do with ethics or people's behavior; the other is to emphasize the humanity of Jesus so much that He has no authority for us. This is done especially by some critical modern scholars. They can argue with great detail why it is that Jesus' example, Jesus' suffering love and cross have nothing to do with how we ought to behave in the world. Jesus thought the world was going to end in a few weeks. Now obviously, if you are not planning for the next generation, you don't have to save any money. If you do not expect the world to be around very long, you will not have to care whether the Romans or somebody else is going to rule. In other words, you pay little attention to the world if you are apocalyptic. You worry less about the problems of social continuity. But now we know of course that the kingdom didn't come; so now we have to keep this old ship going.

Furthermore, Jesus was a rural character. He talked with farmers about the lilies of the field and the sparrows in the bush and all of this beautiful pastoral imagery. Jesus made all morality a matter of face-to-face relationships like those of two farmers who know each other very well. Jesus' principles supposedly then have nothing to say to a modern urban world with all its power politics and its great masses of people that you never get to know. Then of course in addition, Jesus and the early church lived before Constantine, in a time when the church couldn't possibly think about its duties to run the world. There weren't enough Christians around that any of them would be asked to provide social leadership, and of course, since then that changed.

Thus since Jesus was apocalyptic and pre-Constantinian, and a farmer to boot, His example and His moral teachings just are not for our modern world, where we are in control as Christians—you can't get elected president of the United States if you aren't a Christian—where we know the world isn't going to end in the next couple of months through some kind of second coming, and where we know that most people live in the city and we don't know what a lily of the fields is anymore.

This argument makes very good sense theologically to a certain type of person, but ultimately it means that Jesus' humanity is so far from our humanity that it has nothing to say to us. And this, the ancient church ultimately recognized, is the heresy of denying that Jesus was revelatory authority for man.

In between these two heresies, classic Christian orthodoxy has always said that the authority of Jesus and the humanity of Jesus are to be taken at full value, and therefore the kind of humanity it was, the kind of life He lived, and what He did with the problem of evil and enmity, namely, to give Himself for His enemies, is our rule. Because God is a God who gives Himself for His enemies, this is also to be our human response.

11/ BY FRANK H. EPP

The Unilateral Disarmament of the Church

God's goal for humanity is a world without war, without the instruments of war, and without the mentality of war. He has registered this goal as an eternal hope within the human breast and as a recurrent theme in the literature of the human race. One of the most stirring of such passages in the Hebrew-Christian writings is Isaiah's vision of a universal reign of peace and justice:

> It shall come to pass in the latter days that the mountain of the house of the Lord shall be established as the highest of the mountains, and shall be raised above the hills [including Capitol Hill in Washington and Parliament Hill in Ottawa]; and all the nations shall flow to it . . . and they shall beat their swords into plowshares, and their spears into pruning hooks; nation shall not lift up sword against nation, neither shall they learn war any more. (Isaiah 2:2-4)

This projection of the nations of the world actually subjecting their nationalist ambitions to the will of the sovereign God and governing by His light has its parallels in the New Testament literature, notably in the Book of Revelation. In his vision John saw the national societies surrendering their pride and their glory and finding true healing and freedom in such subordination to the throne of God. The extra-scriptural examples of this vision are too numerous to mention, since they can be found both among primitive peoples and more sophisticated societies. Henry Wadsworth Longfellow, for instance, recorded the following Indian version of Isaiah's dream:

> Buried was the bloody hatchet;
> Buried was the dreadful war-club;
> Buried were all war-like weapons,
> And the war-cry was forgotten.
> There was peace among the nations.

Among the more modern countries of Europe in the seventeenth, eighteenth, and nineteenth centuries an impressive number of individuals and societies brought forth internationalist peace proposals to rid Europe of the scourge of war. Most of their ideas were related to Isaiah and John, who, as we have already seen, saw the nations linked together by a common bond, the gospel being the supreme law, and mediation being substituted for war. Men like William Penn, John Bellers, the Abbe Saint-Pierre, Jeremy Bentham, Immanuel Kant, and Leo Tolstoy concerned themselves with plans for international organization.

Such sentiments were not only expressed by the philosopher-writers, but they were also taken seriously by statesmen of the leading late nineteenth-century powers. No less than twenty-six states sent representatives to the first Hague Peace Conference called in 1899 by Nicholas II for the express purpose of discussing disarmament. Although the Russian emperor was motivated in part by his financial and industrial inability to keep up with the European arms race, and though little was achieved at that conference, it did lead to the founding of the International Court of Justice at the Hague. It also became the first of a long series of international conferences on disarmament and peace on which the hopes of mankind would like to ride today.

Problem and Opportunity

The problem of the twentieth century, however, is that we have perfected the weapons of war, multiplied their use in global con-

127

flict, and found no way of disengaging ourselves in spite of the assistance of such instruments as the United Nations. Indeed, we find ourselves confronted with an annual worldwide expenditure of $172 billion for defense systems, with the United States of America spending nearly half that amount alone. At the heart of the arsenal being produced are the nuclear weapons of which a special UN Task Force of Nuclear Arms Escalation recently reported the following:

> There is one inescapable and basic fact. It is that the nuclear armories which are in being already contain large megaton weapons, every one of which has a destructive power greater than that of all the conventional explosive that has ever been used in warfare since the day gunpowder was discovered. Were such weapons ever to be used in numbers, hundreds of millions of people might be killed, and civilization as we know it, as well as organized community life, would inevitably come to an end in the countries involved in the conflict. Many of those who survived the immediate destruction . . . would suffer from long-term effects of irradiation and transmit to their offspring a genetic burden which would become manifest in the disabilities of later generations. ("The Nuclear Time Bomb," *Saturday Review*, December 9, 1967, pp. 70-75)

Every effort to halt the armaments race and to bring about even modest disarmament on a lasting basis has failed. It is true that there were temporary disarmaments. Germany was disarmed after World War I. In 1921-22 France, Italy, Japan, Great Britain, and the United States agreed to limit the number, size, and guns of their battleships for fifteen years. In 1930 Japan, Great Britain, and the United States consented to limit the size and guns of their cruisers, destroyers, and submarines. But it is also true that Germany began to rearm in 1933 and the other agreements lasted only until 1936, as all efforts of the League of Nations disarmament conferences failed. We now know the consequences.

The peace treaties of World War II again provided for the disarmament of certain nations, but general disarmament became even more problematic than after the first world war. The United Nations General Assembly set up a 12-nation Disarmament Commission in 1952, enlarging it to twenty-six members in 1957 and to the full UN membership in 1959. The membership expansion brought the advantage of universal involvement and the disadvantages of limited efficiency and achievement.

Since the early 1960's smaller international groups, such as the 18-nation committee created in 1962, have been meeting periodically to work on the problem. Some nations have created their own task forces, such as the United States Arms Control and Disarmament Agency set up in 1961. All have made little progress, mainly for the reason that Canadian Prime Minister Lester B. Pearson cited when he accepted the Nobel Peace Prize: ". . . we prepare for war like precocious giants, for peace like retarded pygmies. . . ."

Yet, the nations could not relax their efforts entirely. Frightened by the monster which they were creating and prodded by leading scientists of the Pugwash Movement and by a 1958 petition, which bore the signature of 11,000 scientists from forty countries, including thirty-six Nobel Prize winners and thirty-five Fellows of the Royal Society, they kept on working and with some results. In 1963 the USA and the USSR signed the Nuclear Test Ban Treaty prohibiting nuclear weapons tests in the atmosphere, in outer space, and under water. In 1966 the United Nations General Assembly adopted a treaty on principles governing the activities of states in the exploration and use of outer space and specifically banning the orbiting of "any objects carrying nuclear weapons or any other kinds of weapons of mass destruction." This "demilitarization of outer space" treaty was signed simultaneously in London, Moscow, and Washington on January 27, 1967.

Early in 1968 the USA and USSR agreed on a non-proliferation treaty, which is seen by them as a significant arms control measure. Since the treaty, however, does not provide for nuclear stockpile reduction by the super-powers, it is seen by other powers as an attempt to deny them what the USA and USSR are not really willing to give up themselves. Hence, it is difficult for the world community to accept the treaty. So the arms race continues with no end in sight.

Since multilateral or bilateral disarmament appears to be out for reasons of international politics and national pride, some pacifist spokesmen have suggested unilateral disarmament to whichever nation has the wisdom and courage to accept the challenge. However, such acceptance appears to be an unlikely possibility, the proposal being viewed as impractical, although it must still be demonstrated that multilateral rearmament is more practical. The UN Task Force at least has come to the conclusion that the nuclear arms escalation is only increasing insecurity and unendingly complicating the problems it was meant to solve.

In spite of its unpopularity, "impracticability," and "impossibility," as the politicians would say, unilateralism appears to be the call of the hour. If humanity cannot collectively do what is necessary to prevent the ultimate in the destruction of God's creation, then individuals or groups of individuals must move out alone to represent in word and in deed the vision of a disarmed world. And preposterous as the suggestion may seem to the worldly-wise, such an approach isn't really that far out. After all, common sense alone suggests that outright rejection of the present military madness could be quite reasonable.

Besides, the history of mankind supports this approach, for much progress came by way of unilateralism. The human race moved ahead when individuals or groups carried forward with determination and perseverance an idea or a cause which did not have wide popular support. The present causes of majorities were always first the causes of minorities.

Unilateralism also finds its support in Christian theology. Again and again, God and His prophets have acted unilaterally to save the people. Again and again the people have rejected the prophets. But this has not prevented God from acting again. He sent His Son, and that sending was another unilateral act of love. Similarly, the Son's obedient coming was a unilateral act of faithfulness to the will of the Father. Seen by the worldly-wise, Jesus was a fool, of course, because His views and manner of life took Him to the cross. Today we acknowledge, however, that it was precisely the unilateral risk which He took and the sacrifice that He made, which contributed to the salvation of the world.

Jesus was followed in His approach by a small band of disciples, which He had recruited and instructed, and by the church, which they founded. It was only a small flock, a minority movement, but because of its faithfulness to the kingdom idea, it was nevertheless ". . . a chosen race, a royal priesthood, a holy nation, God's own people . . ." (1 Peter 2:9).

The church was always meant to be God's avant-garde, the innovator of His kingdom, the pioneer of the new order. Though the church failed its Lord many times, at its best it could never accept sin, disease, illiteracy, poverty, slavery, injustice, and inequality. At its best it could never accept war. Countless times its members followed Jesus into persecution and martyrdom rather than give up an idea. Its first concern was not that which appeared to be effective, that which was politically expedient, that which brought economic security, but rather that which represented the kingdom. At its best, the church was a unilateral expression on earth of the will of God as it was in heaven.

This is the church's calling also today. As the carrier of Isaiah's vision, as an extension of the body of Christ, and as an international community, the church, more than any other agency, is in position to give to the world the unilateral witness that is needed. Ideally the church is free from all those things which prevent disarmament: the need to satisfy national pride, the need to be economically secure, the need to physically survive. The church doesn't have to be secure and doesn't have to survive. It is free to do God's bidding. Moreover, the church's specialty is to bring about change, first where it matters most in the inner man. As the military machine arises from a military mind, so disarmament issues from the disarmed heart.

What is true in theory is not always true in practice, and regrettably the church has often lost its vision, as it became involved with the ambitions of this world and the struggle for security. Following an early emphasis on pacifism, the Christian church learned to accept the theory of the just war, to bless the Crusades, to promote the wars of religion, and finally to undergird the wars of the respective nation-states, as Roland H. Bainton has reported in his *Christian Attitudes Toward War and Peace* (1960).

Today the warlike stance of the Christian community is attested to in a number of ways. The Canadian Peace Research Institute has discovered "that Christians are more warlike in their attitudes than non-Christians." The *New York Times* assumes that the majority of an estimated 400,000 clergymen of various faiths in the country believe in the righteousness of the Vietnam cause and that the president should push for more than a stalemate (February 11, 1968). C. Wright Mills makes the observation that religion has in all these matters become a subordinate part of the overdeveloped national society. He has said in his "Pagan Sermon to the Christian Clergy":

If there is one safe prediction about religion in this society, it would seem to be that if tomorrow official spokesmen were to proclaim XYZ-ism, next week 90 percent of religious declaration would be XYZ-ist. At least in their conforming rhetoric, religious spokesmen would reveal that the new doctrine did not violate those of the church. As a social and as a personal force, religion has become a dependent variable. It does not originate; it reacts. It does not denounce; it adapts. It does not set forth new models of conduct and sensibility; it imitates. . . . The verbal Christian belief in the sanctity of human life has not of course been affected by the impersonal barbarism of twentieth-century war. But this belief does not itself enter decisively into the plans now being readied for World War III. A savage politician once asked how many divisions the pope had—and it was a relevant question. No one need ask how many chaplains any army that wants them has. The answer is: as many as the generals and their other satraps feel the need of. Religion has become a willing spiritual means and a psychiatric aide of the nation-state. (*The Nation*, March 8, 1958)

The problem of the arms race is complicated by the church's participation, which in turn makes it difficult to respond to present opportunity. The armament race presents an opportunity for the church but the worldwide mood for disarmament and against war doubles that opportunity. The first results of an international poll on disarmament undertaken in France, Poland, and Norway under the sponsorship of UNESCO illustrate that the majority of people believe their governments are spending enough or should be spending less on military defense and also that a majority could approve of the integration of part of their armed forces into a permanent UN international force. In America the aforementioned 20 percent is also not as insignificant as may be believed. After all, the doves include leading teachers, clergymen, women, students, lawyers, economists, architects, engineers, planners, businessmen, artists, writers, actors, and social workers from all over the country. In other words, a not unfavorable national and international climate for a brave unilateral witness exists. The question arises, How can the church, or even just a minority within the church, rise to the occasion and seize the opportunity of the hour?

Liberation and Reorientation

As one surveys the weaknesses of the church, it appears that God's minority movement would be strengthened if it could experience a thoroughgoing psychological and economic liberation, on the one hand, and a theological and political reorientation, on the other hand.

Like the rest of our society, the church is beset by fear. Government-sponsored surveys show that 82 percent of Americans sleep behind locked doors and 37 percent have guns in their homes for protection. And the whole nation is armed to the teeth because of its security. The 1968 State of the Union message called for more cops and guns even for the domestic situation. That a man who had no God and no sense of immortality should feel insecure is clear to us, but we are a society whose testimony is "In God We Trust." Or has that testimony been replaced by the blessing: "Sleep well tonight, your national guard is awake!" an actual message on Minnesota billboards earlier in the decade?

Albert Camus has said that while "the seventeenth century was the century of mathematics, the eighteenth century that of the physical sciences, and the nineteenth century that of biology, our twentieth century is the century of fear." Admitting that to be so, most of us will be inclined to find the cause of our fears outside of ourselves. And well there may be objective reasons for our fear, but the main reasons are subjective. Our fears arise not from the external enemy being so great as that our internal resources are so small. Fear fills the vacuums in our life created by the loss of faith, by the fading of love, the extinction of hope, the retreat of knowledge, and the absence of humility. Fear accompanies doubt, hate, hopelessness, ignorance, pride, and dishonesty. Our fears are the fears of a rich man who has more than his share of the world's wealth, the fears of the guilty running away from the law and from God, the fears of the selfish unwilling to share when conscience tells them they must. Much of the fear we blame on communists actually originates with our consciences.

Is there then no communism to be afraid of? Let us assume for the moment that communism is a real and objective cause for fear. Even so we should remember that superior virtue could cast out the fear brought about by the vices of others. Now what does that mean? you may ask. It means, in the first place, that perfect humility could cast out our fear. If we could admit that communism is a judgment on the church and by that admission judge ourselves, we would not be so fearful of the judgment of communism. Perfect humility would cast out our fear. In the second place, perfect honesty could cast out fear. Honesty would help us to acknowledge that communism for all its ruthlessness has meant an improvement in the living conditions of the masses, and that the church in the Soviet Union does have greater vitality than the church in North America. Perfect honesty would eliminate a good many of our fears. And in the third place, the perfection of our knowledge could cast out our fear, for that knowledge would reveal to us that nationalism is eroding the much-assumed communist monolithic structure and that the evils of communism are its own destruction. I repeat, more perfect knowledge would cast out our fear. If it should really become a fact, as many fear, that communists will threaten our families, our properties, and our lives, we could still be victorious. Perfect love for the communists, perfect faith in God, and a perfect hope of continuing life would take away our fears.

It is urgent for the times in which we live that at least the believers should be liberated from their fears. The man filled with fear soon becomes a terror for others. The man without fear is the truly disarmed man. Jesus spent a considerable part of His time teaching His disciples that the man of faith should be free from fear. He should not fear a hostile environment and not a hostile humanity. He should not even fear persecution and death.

It goes without saying that a faith even as small as a grain of mustard seed could give us more security than the mountains of weapons we have stockpiled. Disarmament begins with a liberation from our fears, and a witness against armament can only proceed from people who have been saved from fear. God wants to save us now and make us so courageous that we can go through the fire for Him.

I have a suspicion that much of the American fear is the fear of the rich man tied to his wealth. Liberation from fear, therefore, really means liberation from poverty. Both are absolute prerequisites for unilateral disarmament. To be freed from fear and to be freed from property is to be freed from dependence on the military. To be freed from such dependence is to have been internally, unilaterally disarmed.

Our liberation from property could begin with a new concept of property. One area in which the new morality of God has made very little difference on the old morality of man's tradition and jungle law is in the area of property. In many other areas we

135

have assumed that the law of the land is not necessarily the law of God, but not with respect to property. In this we have not risen above the law of the land. Our present law has two dimensions: one primitive and the other quite sophisticated. The primitive part says that if you seize a given property and hold it by force, it is yours. By that law Canadians and Americans have made the North American continent their own. The more sophisticated part says that if you can secure legal title to a property by paying for it what is required and agreed upon, it is also your own.

Both of these concepts of property are devoid of any high morality. There is no hint of stewardship in them whatsoever. Yet the law of God relates all property to stewardship, because "the earth is the Lord's and the fulness thereof, the world and those who dwell therein . . .," which is another way of saying that the world and all its resources belong to all of humanity. If a man is set over a property, he is, by the law of God, set over it as a steward. In the eyes of God, the property is man's only as long as he does not exploit it and horde it at the expense of the rest of humanity, present and future. Even the children of Israel, who were told that Canaan was being given to them "forever," were told that "forever" ended with disobedience. Possession was tied to covenant and covenant implied stewardship. Israel as a steward had a responsibility both toward the land and toward the neighbors. Perpetual ownership was guarded against by the law of redistribution which was applied every fifty years.

Measured by this higher law of property we of the West stand condemned. Our polluted soil, water, and air witness to the fact that we are robbing our children. The familiar commentary, "The rich get richer and the poor get poorer," is witness to the fact that we are robbing our world neighbors. Our expenditures for defense are witness to the fact that we are robbing everybody. All our transactions may be legal, and by that standard lawful, but they could by another standard be awfully immoral. In the law courts of God, the biggest thieves may not be the poor who seize what isn't their own by means of riots and revolution but the rich who have kept what isn't their own by craftiness and the protection of the courts. In God's sight we have lost "title" the moment we have taken for ourselves more than our share. And this taking has happened in many ways: by immoral investment, by selfish protectionism, by ruthless military action, and by inadequate giving.

We need to be set free so that our needs will decrease and our defenses will become obsolete. God can set us free and He will set us free if we will let Him. He may have to take away our treasures but that will make us rich toward God. He may have to ask us to sell all that we have, but it will be one way, perhaps the only way, of saving our soul. He says to us through His Son, Jesus:

> Therefore I tell you, do not be anxious about your life, what you shall eat, nor about your body, what you shall put on. . . . For all the nations of the world seek these things; and your Father knows that you need them. Instead, seek his kingdom, and these things shall be yours as well. Fear not, little flock, for it is your Father's good pleasure to give you the kingdom. Sell your possessions, and give alms; provide yourselves with purses that do not grow old, with a treasure in the heavens that does not fail, where no thief approaches and no moth destroys. For where your treasure is, there will your heart be also. (Luke 12:22-34)

Our acceptance of a new concept of property will already be the beginning of the needed theological reorientation. There are probably a number of areas in which rethinking and reformulation are necessary, but crucial to our present problem is the idea of the kingdom of God as our goal, on the one hand, and the cross as a method of achieving it, on the other hand.

Again, we must come back to the visions of Isaiah and John, and to the clear implications of Jesus' role as a King and of His prayer, "Thy kingdom come, thy will be done, on earth as it is in heaven." All of these remind us of the goal which is that "the kingdoms of this world . . . . [are to become] the kingdoms of our Lord, and of his Christ" (Revelation 11:15).

This means that the kingdom really embraces all the world and all of its little kingdoms be they personal, social, commercial, or political. All must be brought under the lordship of Christ, who for that reason is called King of kings. The Wise Men from the East recognized Him as a king; Herod feared Him as a king; the authorities crucified Him as a king; and His followers crowned Him as a king. The Reformation leader, Menno Simons, constantly referred to Him as the Emperor of emperors, or the chief among emperors, thereby clearly placing the authority of Christ in the political context of the time.

Thus to acknowledge Christ and His kingdom is not to have achieved its complete victory, but it means to have made a beginning. Once the kingdom of God is within us it can become something outside of us. Once it is within us, we have given the kingdom a beginning, and we can pray for its coming and its appearance in fullness.

In word and deed, in life and in death, Jesus taught that the way to bring in the kingdom was by way of the cross. To Him the cross was a way of life as well as a gate to the crown of the kingdom. He was frequently heard to say:

> The Son of man must suffer many things. . . . . For the man who wants to save his life will lose it, but the man who loses his life for my sake will save it.

Thus, the cross is both an involuntary suffering resulting from the resistance of the world's kingdoms, and a voluntary experience of suffering. Voluntarily, unilaterally the disciple disarms by accepting the cross. He denies his rights for others. He accepts injustice so that the cause of justice may be advanced. He faces persecution if this is necessary for truth to have its witness. He allows himself to be killed so that the vicious cycle of war is broken. He accepts crucifixion, because it is better that the innocent die for the sins of the people, than that the innocent destroy the people.

This new way of looking at the kingdom and the cross inevitably brings about a new way of looking at the empire and at the gun. In other words, a theological reorientation brings about a political sensitization, or to say it differently yet, the life of a disciple leads to the role of a prophet.

Suddenly the assumption that our government is on God's side and that God is on our government's side becomes questionable. Suddenly we discover the extent to which our American way of life has strayed away from the kingdom and the extent to which American sovereignty has challenged the sovereignty of Christ. Suddenly we wake up to the fact that government is against God when it insists on national sovereignty, on economic protectionism, when it misuses its vast resources, depends for physical and spiritual security on military power, when it enters into unholy alliances, when it mistreats its own and other peoples, and when it tells lies to hide its evil deeds.

Some would call this awakening, this sensitization, a violation of the cherished American concept of separation of church and state. The opposite is true. The emerging prophetic sensitivity and witness is the true essence of separation. And this essence, representing both involvement and separateness, is essential to the work and witness of God's unilaterally disarmed minority movement.

Witness and the Consequences

What shape does the witness take and what are some of the consequences? is probably the next question that emerges. To begin with, we might say that the liberated and reorientated Christian presence is already a part of the witness. To be free from fear and free from property is to be a light in society. To have taken up the cross in pursuit of the kingdom is to be a salt. A significant witness is therefore inherent in unilateral disarmament.

The disarmed Christian has an effect on the American empire in the same way that pacifist Christianity had effect on the Roman Empire, as Edward Gibbons noted: ". . . the introduction of Christianity had some influence on the decline and fall of the Roman Empire . . . the last remnant of the military spirit was buried in the cloisters; a large portion of public and private wealth was consecrated to . . . charity and devotion. . . ."

More needs to be said about the particular forms of the contemporary witness, and one of its dimensions is certainly a resistance to nation-worship. When the US naval officer, Captain Stephen Decatur, and all of his followers, including Cardinal Spellman, repeat the notorious toast, "My country right or wrong," the Christian witness says, "There is no god but God!" Let's face it, nation-worship is as real a temptation for us as it was for the Christians of the Roman Empire and as real as it was for the German Christians during the era of the Third Reich. To give Americanism a Christian halo does not change the fact. A nation is known more by the fruits of its imperialism than by its pious propagandistic claims.

In such a context, the Christian witness has political relevance and content. The followers of the King of kings can no more escape political implications than He could, offending as He was to both the Jews and the Romans. Nor can they escape it any more than Paul could escape it as a preacher of the gospel and as a martyr in Rome. His preaching in Thessalonica had already produced the accusation that he was "acting against the decrees of Caesar, saying that there is another king, Jesus." For faith in America today not to have some political implications would be like faith in the context of affluence not to have some economic implications.

This means that the witness on behalf of the great white throne and Him who sits on it must also have some relevance to the big white house and him who sits in it. Yet there is a widespread notion in our land that the separation of church and state prevents the church from proclaiming the King and His kingdom to the president.

We need only recall the Anabaptist reformer, Menno Simons, whose zeal was always in bad taste and whose sharp tongue always appeared to be rude, to wit:

> When I think to find a magistrate who fears God, who performs his office correctly and uses his sword properly, then verily I find as a general rule nothing but a Lucifer, an Antiochus, or a Nero, for they place themselves in Christ's stead so that their edicts must be respected above the Word of God. Whosoever does not regulate himself according to them and does not serve Baal, but maintains the ceremonies of Christ and lives according to the Word of God, such a one is arrested as a hoodlum and made to suffer his property confiscated. . . . Besides we have their unreasonable pomp, pride, greed, uncleanness, lying, robbing, stealing, burning, hatred, envy, avarice, and idolatry. Yet they want to be called Christian princes and gracious lords. O Lord! . . .

Closely related to the witness in high places and low is the complete disassociation from the military establishment. This can mean many things. It most certainly should mean personal conscientious objection to war and the draft. Since April 1967 it also means that the peace churches are in favor of conscientious objector status for all those who object whatever their reason may be. Perhaps it should also mean, as it has already meant for the Reverend William Sloane Coffin, Jr., and Dr. Benjamin Spock, and three other leaders of the draft resistance movement, counseling young men to violate the Selective Service laws, and engaging in various other acts of civil disobedience.

Christians are normally most anxious to obey the authorities, but they cannot in good conscience do so when the authorities themselves are disobeying God. Almost every major Christian theologian (Tertullian, Origen, Augustine, Wycliffe, Luther, Calvin, and Aquinas) has held that under certain circumstances it is right for Christians to resist the civil authorities, believing like Peter that "we must obey God rather than men." J. R. Burkholder has expressed the opinion that the urgency of the present situation calls for "radical pacifism." By this term he refers—

> . . . to movements of noncooperation and nonviolent direct action which go beyond the areas of nonresistant witness usually considered legitimate by the historic peace churches. Noncooperation includes refusal to pay taxes for military purposes, to obey civil defense regulations, and to cooperate with selective service. Direct action refers to protests and acts of civil disobedience. . . .

Disassociation should also mean non-dependence on the military for protection, particularly if this means the execution of any number of other people, and also the refusal to accept a military crusade on the grounds that it represents protection and extension of the gospel. Is there not something very terrible about Western troops rescuing Western missionaries in the Congo by shooting hundreds of blacks? Has the time not come for Christians to insist that in their service abroad their lives are no more precious than the lives of the people they have come to serve, not in need of any greater security and protection, and not always in need of evacuation every time the red alert goes on? As Menno Simons has said:

> Our weapons are not weapons with which cities and countries may be destroyed, walls and gates broken down, and human blood shed in torrents like water. But they are weapons with which the spiritual kingdom of the devil is destroyed and the wicked principle in man's soul is broken down: We have and know no other weapons, besides this, the Lord knows, even if we should be torn into a thousand pieces, and if as many false witnesses rose up against us as there are spears in the fields, and grains of sand upon the seashore.

The consequences of the bold proclamation and the radical witness, of course, are clear. Those who unreservedly and unilateral-

142

ly disarm and commit themselves to the vision of Isaiah and the kingdom of our Lord must expect insult, outrage, suffering, and harassment. Society will forsake them. Some popular preachers will denounce them. The FBI will watch them. The military will pursue them. And the courts will jail them. As the crisis deepens, some may even be charged with treason and put to death. Yet, as those who were persecuted before them, they will have the satisfaction and the joy of giving continuity to Isaiah's vision, of contributing to a warless world, of bringing in the kingdom. By faith they know that posterity will call them blessed and that they will hear the Lord saying, "Well done, good and faithful servant."

Conclusion

Perhaps the best way to sum up all that has been said is to report another fact from Jesus' life, namely, that there came a time for Him to "set his face to go to Jerusalem." He could have found a hundred reasons for not going. There was so much to be done up-country. So many people to be helped. Besides there was peace and quiet, and in Galilee He even had a few friends left. He set His face to go to Jerusalem, for He knew there was no other way to accomplish His mission. The religious, commercial, military, and governmental authorities had to be confronted with the King and the kingdom. He knew, of course, that He would be sentenced to die. He also knew that the cross would be the key to the kingdom. Similarly, some years later Paul set his face to go to Rome. In our century there came a time for the German Christians to set their face to go to Berlin. Only a few obeyed. Now the time has come for the disciples in America to set their face on Washington. It is impossible to turn away and still be true to Jesus, and, we might add, to the best interests of America.

12/ BY J. LAWRENCE BURKHOLDER

The Church in a Brave New World

The problem of building the church in the brave new world is twofold: How? And why? Of the two, the latter is the most pressing. It is pressing because one of the implications of the world's bravery is its independence from the church. The brave new world is a secular world of technological power which has learned to get along without the church. The most pressing problem is therefore how to convince the world that it needs the church; indeed, this is not so much a problem of the world as a problem of the church itself. Does the church have anything which the world needs?

The new world has bravely declared, at least by implication, that much that the church has offered in the past is no longer needed. The church has offered a world view based upon the supernatural. But most people of the brave new world have abandoned the concept of the supernatural without an overwhelming sense of loss. The church has offered a metaphysical framework within which to view the whole of reality, but the brave new world is brave in the sense that it is no longer interested in metaphysical systems. The church has offered a view of nature based upon the conception of Creation, but nature reveals her secrets through scientific investigations rather than through religious myths; the church has offered a view of the good society based upon religious imagery, but society in the brave new world is held together by "socio-technical" controls. The brave new world is not opposed to religion; it just sees no point in it.

Certainly times have changed since the days when Christianity could view itself as being wiser than the pagan world. When Christendom was formed, all wisdom and knowledge was contained within the church—both scientific and religious. The church was the possessor of the knowledge of God and of the world. The barbarians were ignorant as well as pagan. All knowledge was integrated by theology and the church had authority over secular institutions. Kings even stood barefoot in the snow before religious leaders. But now the church as such knows very little about anything that concerns the world. The church is an authority only within the realm of religion. And this has become detached from knowledge in general. The knowledge of nature, man, history, and society is gained independently of the church, and when the church attempts to dictate to the secular realm, it does so at considerable risk.

A Modest Church

All this means, therefore, that the church in the brave new world will be a modest church. It will be modest not because of self-doubt, but rather because it is no longer in a position to call the plays as it was 500 years ago. Natural science, psychology, politics, social sciences, and historical investigation are in the saddle of change. The church is, therefore, "displaced" and to a large extent it is no longer a vital factor in the affairs of men.

The massiveness, as well as the independence, of the world is astonishing. One needs only to stand in central Manhattan to see symbolized the relative power of the church and worldly institutions. Modern skyscrapers with glass sides symbolize the technological revolution together with vast economic power. Here decisions are made which determine the social and economic life of the nation. The church by comparison is a feeble institution; its spires no longer rule the sky and few people attend church in the inner city.

Furthermore Christendom is now past. As Mennonites, we helped to destroy it. We opposed the organic unity of church and

145

society for the sake of a pure church. But there were at the same time secular forces at work which resulted in the breakdown of religion in society at large. The secularization of corporate life resulted. Separation of church and state led unwittingly to separation of religion from life. Economic institutions, education, communication, welfare were separated from the church. To be sure, various sects attempted from time to time to establish their own culture, especially under agrarian conditions, but now these are being swallowed up by the "secular city." The church, therefore, has no organic claim on the world. The world is free to create its own future. Once the question was, "By what right can the world be free of ecclesiastical control?" Now the question is, "By what right can the church intervene in the life of the world?"

This problem, posed by the breakdown of Christendom and the secularization of society, of course, loses its force if the work of the church is limited to individual conversions and the cultivation of person piety. In this case, the form or structure of society at large is not envisaged as the legitimate problem of the church. If our approach to the world is pietistic, it makes little or no difference that the world is a brave new world. Its bravery makes no difference, since the church is built by adding members one by one. The pietistic church makes an unwritten concordat with society to let society pursue its corporate life unhindered in exchange for non-interference by the state. But at the same time it needs to be pointed out that erstwhile pietists have frequently become the most adamant defenders of the status quo, who tend to move from an apolitical piety to political conservatism.

Pietism, of course, contains within it a permanently valid emphasis. It stands for the necessity of personal religious experience. Grace is individually experienced and personal sanctification is an essential part of the Christian life. Any adequate approach to the brave new world must include the permanent insight of pietism into the nature of the Christian life. Pietism, however, is blind to the influence of social structures upon the Christian community. It has no critical capacity for judging the overall influence of social change upon the Christian life. It fails to realize that Christians are part of a total order, and that the Christian life will reflect the total order despite renunciation of personal vices such as drinking and smoking.

A Servant Church

What should be the fundamental stance of the church to the world? It should be the stance of the servant. The church must serve the world. It must bind up the wounds of the brave new world. Ironically, the brave new world is a sick and bleeding world. For alongside unparalleled prosperity and higher education, travel, and technology, lies misery, poverty, mental illness, race prejudice, revolution, war, personal anxiety, guilt, and marital discord. One suspects that there is something a bit fraudulent about the brave new world. It is a world teetering on the brink of disaster. It is a twisted and distorted world in which wisdom and power are less than coefficient. It is a world of vast dislocations and contradictions. Hence, the apparent independence and self-confidence of the brave new world is illusory. The brave new world as well as the secular city cannot escape the fact of original sin. Indeed, the proximity of widespread affluence and grinding poverty is proof that sin is a factor which is constant in human existence.

Although the servant church will maintain its integrity as a religious fellowship with its own inner life, it will humbly seek to meet the needs of the world. Gone are the days of imperial majesty when ecclesiastical symbols were derived from royal power. The crown, the scepter, golden vessels, and ermine surplices are simply out of character. The church must wear humble garb and be willing to identify with people of low estate. Identification means suffering with the less fortunate. It may mean becoming poor, taking on the condition of the underprivileged, sharing their life and experiencing their discomfiture. The church must become an institution for the world without becoming an institution of the world. Indeed, the only way the church can cease to be of the world is to be for the world. The way churches become of the world these days is to live for themselves in the same way that people live for themselves. My

147

feeling is that a great historic change must come over the church. Instead of regarding its own growth, grandeur, and universal power as its historical goal, it must regard the well-being of the world as its reason for existence.

Historically, the church has not assumed the role of the servant; rather, it has assumed the role of the ruler. Somehow, the church for over 1,000 years has failed to distinguish between the regal and servant imagery in the New Testament. Jesus is presented in the New Testament as "Lord." Indeed, according to Matthew 28, "all power in heaven and earth belongs to Jesus." The post-resurrection formula for Jesus was regal. Nevertheless, the early church did not deduce from this that the church reigns with Him at this time, though it may anticipate rule with Christ in the eschaton. The model for the church of the New Testament remained the earthly life of Jesus, "who came not to be ministered unto, but to minister." The man who was born in a stable, who served His people, and who died on a cross at a dump heap is the prototype of the church. Until the end, the earthly Christ is the Model—not the resurrected Christ who possesses all power and authority. The great error of the church has been the gradual appropriation of regal and heavenly attributes to itself. This is the root of Christendom. This is the reason why there developed a theory of the church's supremacy over the state. The idea that Christ is Lord has been construed to mean that the church is His instrument for rule over the world.

What is wrong with this view is that it presupposes a false eschatology. It is an eschatology which attributes to the church powers which belong to it only in the eschaton. Until Christ comes again, the model for the church as an earthly fellowship is Jesus of Nazareth—not Jesus the heavenly Lord. One would have to conclude that the approach of the church to the world throughout most of history has been what Robert McAfee Brown calls a "false witness." It has given the impression on the basis of its own arrogance, power, and royal pretensions that the nearest analogy to Christ is political dominion. For most of Christian history there has been a contradiction between the life and message of Jesus Christ and the church's fundamental position. The church is not intended to rule. It is intended to witness and to help. Therefore, one can readily see that the building of great church buildings and hierarchical systems is fundamentally wrong. I do not have traditional Catholicism in mind only, but even evangelical churches who, despite their voluntaryism, are jealous of their influence in the community, and make the building of the church by adding convert to convert a means for their own glorification.

Practically speaking, churches will increasingly take on the character of service agencies. The church will become the place where certain unmet spiritual, psychological, and social needs are met. This does not replace worship, evangelism, pastoral care. It simply means that all that the MCC and the mission boards have stood for in the past will need to be combined in the local church. So far as congregational activities are concerned, it means development both of professional and nonprofessional ministries.

A Prophetic Church

Another feature of the church in the brave new world will be its prophetic responsibility. The brave new world will need to be reminded of its sins. Its power is likely to tempt it to arrogance. Its rapidity of change is bound to leave unfortunate victims behind. Its institutional character may make true freedom difficult, if not impossible. Its artificiality may lead to inhumanity, and its technological prowess may result in an exploitative attitude toward nature. But prophecy requires intelligence as well as courage. Prophecy today means that the prophet must take on the brave new world in argument. This means that the church must be informed about the world. The content of prophecy cannot consist only of general moral principles, but also proposals with some degree of specificity. Insofar as they become specific, they must meet the demands of political reality. Therefore, prophets must know something about the world to whom they prophesy.

If the church is to influence the shape of the brave new world, it must find ways to harness Christian intelligence. This does not mean that all intelligent Christians must work in church institutions. It does mean, however, that new forms of communication must be created between Christians—even nominal Christians— and the church. If the church is to speak and act wisely, it must see the world through the eyes of sociologists, political scientists, and psychologists, as well as through the eyes of theologians. Unless the church somehow ties in with secular sources, it will find itself completely alienated from the decision-making processes of the world. No matter how right the church may be in its espousal of eternal principles of right, it will speak in effectively, indeed it will not find the confidence to speak unless it is able to speak with technical competence.

The prophetic role of the church is not merely to call attention to injustices in society, but to help to set forth goals for humanity. The great question today is this: What is the good life? What kind of life does God will for man? This is a theological question, but it is also a question that lies underneath the planners of this age. Statesmen, politicians, scientists, if they will meet their responsibilities for the future, must answer this question. Is man intended to live in a totally artificial order such as the modern city? Or is man intended to be directly related to nature? Does man need privacy? How much change can man tolerate? What provision needs to be made for man's participation in the arts? What is a minimum standard of living? To what extent does human fulfillment depend upon fulfillment of the entire human race? In whose hands does human destiny belong? And, of course, new ethical problems will have to be answered. Shall life be created in the laboratory? How far will man be permitted to go in genetic manipulation? Shall births be controlled legally? Shall the state continue to maintain the right to draft men to kill and be killed in its defense? These and other questions are facing the world as it enters into a new age of technological power. These are precisely the questions facing the world, and the church will take a back seat in the brave new world unless it is competent to understand them and to make concrete proposals which make sense.

Understanding the world realistically does not mean that the church will necessarily take a soft attitude toward the world. There will be points at which the church will have to make a complete break. I see ahead a complete reassessment of war by Christians. Christians may also have to break with the tax structure. The man in Massachusetts who refused to turn his eighteen-year-old over to the armed forces, arguing that the youth belongs to the parents until he comes of age, is typical of the kind of person that the church will need. Christians may have to fill the jails of the most powerful nation in the world before they can enter the kingdom of heaven. Christians may be faced with the necessity of making a decision between established power and radical revolution in the years ahead as Negroes attempt to make a place for themselves in American society by force. What practical, constructive, redemptive course is open to us who side with the underprivileged in principle and yet refuse to use force? Must we simply sit out the revolution and then send in MCC relief workers, or is there a more constructive role to which God is calling us?

A Reformed Church

I see implicit in the question of the church's responsibility to the brave new world, seeds of disunity which will occasion great strains in the church in the next decades. Fundamental questions are bound to be raised as they already are being raised about the extent and manner to which the church should become involved in the life of the world. Some people see in this a call to obedient witness; others feel that it is beside the point. There are those who feel that the task of the church is to attend to her own affairs as a religious institution or fellowship, perfecting her saints, evangelizing the world one by one through personal conversion, protecting the worldly character of religious institutions, emphasizing personal morality, defending traditional theological language, and building up the life of the religious community. Certainly much can be said for this approach, but I doubt whether it is satisfactory as far as it goes. The problems with it are at least twofold—the one is sociological and the other theological. (1) Sociologically, Christian people these days are so much a part of and dependent upon their world environment that they cannot live a separate existence. The lives we live (internally and externally) are to an increasing extent determined by the social organism of which we are a part. The clothes we wear, the houses we live in, the money we earn, the cars we drive, the goals we share, the images of the world we reflect are to a large extent given to us by society at large—especially as these ideas, ideals, and values are communicated by television and public education. If we are to live useful, godly lives, we must enter into the job of environmental control. For our own salvation and the salvation of our children, we must influence society so that moral ideals are a possibility. (2) Theologically, it is necessary for Christians who seek to worship and to serve God to communicate to the world the will of God, whatever that may be. The will of God, of course, is manifold. It includes belief in Jesus Christ, membership in the body of Christ, but where that is rejected there is yet a word from God which may coincide with the highest and most lofty ideals of secular humanism.

The simple dichotomy of the church and the world, according to which the church speaks to the world as if the world consisted of outsiders, is contrary to the facts. The Christian population of America is so large that when the church speaks to the world it is really speaking at the same time to itself. The opinion of the churches and the opinion of the nation are interlocked. It is a sad reflection upon the churches that what they advocate for the world is frequently superior to what they permit in the churches. The nation reflects the liberal side of their thinking and the church their conservative side. At least this has been the story in civil rights. People generally have been willing to integrate the army and the public schools before the churches. The overlap of the churches and the nation in America means that Christian witness to the world is witness to the church and Christian witness to the church is witness to the world.

A Polyform Church

I would like now to speak about the form of church life in the brave new world. I believe that the external form of the church will be greatly altered in the future. The church will become polyform. The stereotypes of the past will be broken by thousands of experiments in church order and practice, and this, undoubtedly, will cause great tensions within the church. It seems that many church people, particularly the younger generation, are getting tired of the church in its present form.

One great Protestant institution which is being challenged is preaching. There is at the present time a strong reaction against preaching, even among seminarians. They feel that its authoritative stance is out of keeping for this age, and its dependence upon the insights of a single pastor is unrealistic. The time when all or nearly all the people would assemble to hear a sermon may be drawing to a close. People are much more interested in discussion in relatively intimate settings where problems can be worked through by the group. It is true that in certain circles the sermon still draws, but increasing numbers of people who have been brought up on TV find sermons boring. Churches in the future may take on the form of fellowship and teaching centers. In this regard they will resemble synagogues. It is quite possible that in the future congregations will consist of small groups meeting frequently in houses, small chapels, public buildings. Occasionally, possibly once a month, they will all gather together for rallies, celebrations, for evangelistic meetings and preaching. Churchgoing in the future will probably have a somewhat ad hoc character, but its goals will be more specific and meetings will be more intensive. The routinization of Protestant church life will probably give way to a more individualistic approach to congregational life. My prediction is that religion in the future will be less inhibited and more emotional. We will find modern equivalents to the camp meeting and to the revival. Leadership will be increasingly charismatic. Worship, like life in general, will be unsettled and discipleship will become more differentiated as the church itself reflects the cultural pluralism of America.

Although I would not equate the absence of structure with the freedom of the Spirit, I would express the hope that the next age of the church may be an age characterized by the work of the Holy Spirit. Changes in present structures are bound to come and a new freedom is bound to descend upon the churches (Catholic, Protestant, and Mennonite). But the question is whether the new freedom is a belated expression of the individualism of the Renaissance with its emphasis upon the independence of the individual, or whether it is the discovery of a reality beyond man and even beyond the community. All we can do is hope and pray that the unfettering from the past will mean the awareness of the reality of God who is the Author of true freedom.

Conclusion:
Peacemaking in a Broken World

Peacemaking, though a Christian obligation, has often been negated by Christians engaged in combat or by the church vigorously supporting the combatants. This is certainly not strange, for the task of peacemaking demands rare and unusual talents. Genuine peacemaking is an expression of love, nurtured in faith and motivated by hope. The peacemaker or reconciler will speak the truth in love. He will have to understand as well as be understood. He will need to act courageously yet lovingly, boldly yet humbly. Peacemaking, however, is not only the work of individuals but the work of the Christian community—the church.

The brokenness of the world challenges the church in every generation to find new ways of bringing peace and reconciliation. Never has this task been so complex as in our time. The threat of war now includes the possibility of nuclear annihilation. War is no longer the plaything of the generals or the professionals but the mobilization of entire societies which joust for supremacy. The sources of war rise out of inflammations caused by ideological, national, and racial rivalries. Total war exempts no one from its gargantuan influences.

The Christian obligation and the warring world have always lain heavy on the Mennonite conscience. As one of the historic peace churches, Mennonites have been known for their belief in pacifism, or as it is known within the brotherhood, nonresistance. Nonresistance has been a style of life, an attempt to follow Christ in human relationships, rather than a theological formulation or a political strategy. There have, of course, been numerous failures.

This vocation of peace is grounded in the conviction that Jesus taught His followers to be people of peace. The character of this vocation developed through the experiences of persecution and in the isolation of rural life.

This volume attests to the fact that peacemaking continues to be a dynamic concern of the Mennonite Church. But circumstances have forced reconsiderations. Where rural isolation once tended to make nonresistance a matter primarily for the brotherhood itself, the changing styles of modern life along with fresh biblical insights have helped the church to discover anew that discipleship means being "little Christs," to use Martin Luther's phrase, in the world. The search is now for a style of life in what is now one world and where no one is exempt from the militarism of American society.

By no means does this volume discuss all the issues raised on peace and peacemaking. Questions regarding the draft, conscientious objection, war taxes, and formal political action for peace are missing completely. Other issues are given insufficient attention. For instance, how is one nonresistant in a society governed by what President Eisenhower once labeled the "military-industrial complex"? Can one be nonviolent when society itself is organized to destroy the personal freedom of some of its citizenry? From another vantage point, how is one nonresistant in a revolutionary setting? How is one a peacemaker where the established institutions need to be destroyed if justice is to be achieved? Finally, how can one work for world peace when he lives in a rich island surrounded by masses of hungry and starving people?

Peacemaking is a process. There are always unresolved problems and new dilemmas. That in itself brings us to the profoundly Christian stance of waiting for a word from the Lord. Such a word will come as we understand the times, listen to the Holy Spirit, and hear the voices of our brothers. Hopefully these essays will provoke further discussion within the brotherhood, contribute to the search for peace in the worldwide church, and stimulate peacemaking by all men of goodwill. "Happy are those who work for peace among men: God will call them his sons" (Matthew 5:9, TEV)!

Questions for Study and Thought

1. What are the sources of unrest in your community? Are there any ghettos? Who are the local poor? Why are they poor?

2. How are the people of your community related to the city? What benefits do the members of your congregation gain from the nearby city? What do they contribute in return?

3. Investigate what groups are operating in your community which promote extremist viewpoints. Find out if there is a voluntary peace group or human relations unit which may need your help.

4. Construct position papers for your congregation on the war in Vietnam and on housing discrimination in your community. How could your congregation use these statements as an effective witness?

5. How has the Bible been used to support war, racial discrimination, and social inequality? How would you use the Bible to combat racism and nationalism in the church?

6. What are the qualities of life that are essential for a person to be a reconciler in conflict situations? How did Jesus reconcile the extremists and militants of His day? Was He always successful?

7. What kinds of power do the Scriptures sanction? Can the church legitimately use the power she possesses to correct injustice and promote a just society?

8. How does the nonresistant person live and work in the midst of a revolutionary situation? Can the church serve both as innovator and preserver in the social order?

9. Does the use of the legal provision for conscientious objectors constitute an acceptance of a militaristic political order? Should the church become more active in protesting the draft system?

10. The Bible speaks of wars and rumors of war as part of human history. Why then should Christians protest war? What hopes are there that dissent against war contributes to peacemaking?

11. How did the early church serve as a model community in the ancient broken world? How should the church be a model community in today's broken world?

12. What can you do to break down the unconcern for, and the apathy toward, human suffering that exists in your community and in your congregation?

Contributors

Atlee Beechy is professor of education, Goshen College, Goshen, Indiana. He has served as director of Vietnam Christian Service.

Stanley Bohn is pastor of the First Mennonite Church, Bluffton, Ohio.

J. Lawrence Burkholder is Victor S. Thomas Professor of Divinity, Harvard Divinity School.

Richard C. Detweiler is pastor of the Souderton Mennonite Church, Souderton, Pennsylvania.

Peter J. Ediger is pastor of the Mennonite Church, Arvada, Colorado.

Frank H. Epp, Ottawa, Ontario, is on the staff of the Peace Section of Mennonite Central Committee.

C. Norman Kraus is chairman of the Department of Bible and Religion, Goshen College, Goshen, Indiana.

R. Herbert Minnich is associate professor of sociology, Goshen College, Goshen, Indiana.

Hubert Schwartzentruber is pastor of Bethesda Mennonite Church, St. Louis, Missouri.

Sanford G. Shetler is a bishop in the Mennonite Church at Johnstown, Pennsylvania.

Willard Swartley is instructor in Bible and philosophy, Eastern Mennonite College, Harrisonburg, Virginia.

John Howard Yoder is associate director of the Institute of Mennonite Studies, Elkhart, Indiana.

John A. Lapp is associate professor of history, Eastern Mennonite College, Harrisonburg, Virginia.